My Search for the "One Thing"

My Radical Encounters with God while Searching for the "One Thing"

Mark Levesque

Copyright © 2019 Mark Levesque

All rights reserved.

ISBN: 9781070417561

DEDICATION

To my wife Kathy. Thank you for joining me in this journey. It has been such a blessing having you by my side through this adventure. Sharing life with you has been a piece of heaven on earth.

CONTENTS

	Acknowledgments	i
1	Why the "One Thing"?	1
2	Man Made God in His Image	19
3	We All Need to Be Part of Something Big	27
4	The Man Upstairs Came Downstairs	44
5	The Reports of God's Death Have Been Exaggerated	55
6	My Wife and Sons Need Miracles	65
7	My Journey to Heaven and Hell	80
8	The Kingdom of God at Work	98
9	The Kingdom Is Here and Now	109
10	Abundance Is a Way of Thinking	126

ACKNOWLEDGMENTS

The following pages draw from over 40 years of spiritual growth that I received from more mentors and teachers than I have time or space to thank. I would still like to mention a few individuals whose contributions to my personal spiritual development were very significant.

I would like to particularly thank Jerold Buishas, Joe Buishas and Bob May for helping to open my eyes to the unconditional love of God; John Scudder, my first pastor, who introduced me to Jesus Christ and to divine healing when I most needed it; Steve Darr for inspiring me to begin writing this book; and Andrew Wommack and Malcolm Smith, whose teaching ministries have been of immeasurable help to me over the years.

1. WHY THE "ONE THING"?

When I began this journey, I was successful in business but was also miserable. I had everything that I was told would make me happy: a wife and son I adored, a nice home and even a German sports car. So why was I such an emotional and physical wreck?

I was not looking for God or the meaning of life. I was just looking for answers to the problems I was facing. I eventually found the answers I was looking for but not in the way I was expecting at the time.

Later I discovered that God was with me on this journey all along. He taught me some valuable lessons about life through the struggles and experiences that I will be sharing with you in the following chapters.

Looking for the One Thing

Almost everyone wants to live a life that matters. Most people want to know why they are here and what is the purpose and meaning of their life.

In the movie *City Slickers,* the old cowboy Curley, played by Jack Palance, holds up one finger and asks Mitch, played by Billy Crystal, "Do you know what the secret to life is? It's just one thing. You stick to that and nothing else matters." Mitch responds, "That's great, but what's the one thing?" Curley then says, "That's what you've got to figure out!"

That's what this book is about - helping each of us find out the one thing that will give our lives more meaning and purpose. It's pretty radical to be looking for the meaning of life when almost everyone around us is caught up on a treadmill, doing the same things over and over, day after day, and getting nowhere.

The fact that you are reading this book means that either you have something gnawing at your mind saying there's got to be more to life than this or the pain of staying in your current situation has now become worse than the pain of changing. All of this has brought you to the point of asking, "Why am I here?"

I believe that Curley is right about the secret to life. What he doesn't tell us, though, is not only will finding the one thing make a huge difference in our lives, but even the journey itself will make a difference.

This is my story. I haven't told it before, but it is about my radical journey to find the "one thing" and the radical changes this search has made in my life. It's also about inspiring you to radically seek your "one thing" and to raise your expectancy, so as you seek your purpose in life, it may become clearer to you.

Finding the "One Thing" Began at a Funeral

My quest for my "one thing" began at my maternal grandmother's funeral. I had been going to college fulltime in the mornings and working fulltime at a lumber yard. It was long before cell phones so I didn't hear of her passing until late that evening. Her death really hit me hard, and I wept for hours. I was very close to my grandparents. In my early years growing up I lived with my parents and siblings in the same house as my grandparents. Since we lived so close, I spent a lot of time with them, and they had a huge influence on my upbringing.

Their generation lived through the Great Depression and two world wars, which meant that they were very self-reliant and had strong work ethics. These were values that affected me as a youngster as I spent time with my grandmother in the kitchen or with my grandfather working on the car or some project around the house.

My dad was also close to Grandma. His dad was sick for most of his formative years, so his mom had the greatest influence on him. When she died, like me, it really hit him hard.

At the funeral my dad said something to me that stuck in my mind like a splinter that I couldn't remove or get over for years. Right in the middle of his mother's funeral as the priest was proclaiming that she's in a better place in the afterlife, my dad said to me, "I wonder if this is all a sham?" That really caught me by surprise. He was a deacon in his church. He had spent years in training and study and didn't know for certain what happens after we die. Wow!

This one simple question stuck in my mind and drove me to search for answers, which ultimately led me to find my "one thing".

I needed to know what happens after we die. If this life is all there is, then there really isn't any meaning to anything outside of eating, drinking and being merry, and that gets boring pretty fast. However, if we live on after death then everything we do has meaning here and forever. I wanted to know for sure and how to prepare. If we meet God on the other side, what does He want from us and is He here in this life?

A Tale of Two Kingdoms

I eventually found answers to these questions. Some of what I found out was pretty radical. For example, I learned that we not only live on after death but we live here on earth in two worlds, one physical and the other spiritual.

I also discovered that the spiritual world is the source of this physical world and that we can tap into the spiritual world for help in overcoming the cares and problems of this world. These answers helped me begin to realize that my "one thing" is related to knowing that we live in two worlds or kingdoms at the same time. I also began to understand how to tap into the resources of the spiritual world I call the Kingdom of God to help myself and others improve our circumstances here in this physical world that I call the kingdom of earth.

It's seems pretty radical to look to the spiritual realm for help in the natural, but it really does make a difference when we do.

Radical - to Return to the Source

Is God radical, or rad, as the word is used these days? That's an interesting question. So, what is a radical? Is it someone who challenges the status quo, or is it something very different? Actually, the current use of the word *radical* is very different from the usual or traditional meaning.

The original definition of *radical* means relating to, or proceeding from, a root. That is where the word radish comes from because it is the root of that plant. To be radical doesn't mean to pull away from the established order but, rather, to return to the source or root of a thing. Since God is the source or root of everything, He is the ultimate radical in the universe; and everyone who follows Him will become a radical, as well.

Since radical means the root, source or foundation of something, and with God being the primal mover of everything in this world, a true radical is a person who is building their life on the foundational principles that come from the Creator Himself. If something or someone seems radical, in the truest sense of the word, it means that they are returning to the way that things were initially designed and how they should be.

Radical Love

Take love for example. I always knew my parents loved me, but I wasn't sure that my dad liked me. His mom (my grandma) was another story. I always felt she loved and accepted me just the way I was. Her love for me was the closest thing to unconditional love I remember from early childhood.

She never learned to drive so most Saturday mornings we would take long walks downtown to visit the half dozen banks Grandma had accounts with. After depositing her savings for the week, we would stop off at the lunch counter of Grant's Department Store, a New England version of Woolworth's or Wal-Mart, to enjoy ice cream sundaes. I would always get to eat mine and half of Grandma's.

This started my lifelong love affair or addiction to ice cream. I think I love ice cream because I associate it with one of the more enjoyable experiences of childhood. If someone asked me, "Do you love ice cream?", I'd likely say yes! But I don't mean it the way I love my wife or our children!

I discovered that in our culture the word *love* is used quite indiscriminately. The way we talk about love, you might think that we love our parents and partners the same way we love sports or ice cream. This makes it sound like we really don't know what love is, and maybe we don't!

It was much the same way in Jesus' day. Greek was the most widely used language at that time, and there were four primary words for love of which I know. Two of the most widely used in ancient Greek literature and plays were "eros", from which we get our word erotic or physical love, and "phileo", from which we get the word Philadelphia or brotherly love.

Jesus emphasized a different word from the Greek lexicon for His kind of love. This word for love was in the Greek language but never used in any Greek writings that we know of. Jesus introduced the word "agape" in Greek and defined it as divine, unconditional love or care for another.

This was a truly radical concept because Jesus was departing from the human, self-serving concepts of love that were dominant in society in His day. He always pointed people back to "agape", God's kind of love, that gives itself away for the benefit of another.

Knowing these three different distinctions for "love" can make a powerful difference in our lives. Practicing God's kind of love in our daily lives helps us in everything we do, from being more patient with our friends and family to being a better leader at work, school or church.

In this book we will cover several radical concepts about God. This may help you uncover some misconceptions about God that may be limiting you, just as they were limiting me from fulfilling the destiny for which I had been designed.

I will be sharing about a number of personal God encounters and some of the resulting revelations. I am sharing these experiences now because I believe that God wants me to do so. These types of spiritual experiences are not unique to any one person and are available to everyone. I hope that you find my testimony helpful and that hearing my account of what God has done for me will inspire you to seek and *expect* more radical revelations and experiences from Him!

Why Can't You Be Like Everyone Else?

I came into this world at a time when science was supreme. Everything manmade was thought to be superior to nature. Pregnant moms were put to sleep for the delivering of their babies, and my mom was one of them. This was preferable for the pediatrician's schedule but not ideal for mom and baby's health and wellbeing. Years later the medical community discovered that nature had it right all along.

As a young child I was quite insecure. I could blame my childhood feelings of loneliness and inadequacy on the anesthesia or on baby formula, but that would be shortsighted. Since everyone feels this way to some degree, it's probably just part of growing up.

Mom and Dad Did the Best They Could

My early years were spent in a one-bedroom apartment on a busy street in an old New England mill town. Mom and Dad did the best they could. Dad was busy working night and day at his struggling pharmacy so he wasn't around much; and when he was home, he was so stressed we all walked on eggshells, not wanting to do something to set him off. The fact that my parents had seven kids and two foster children meant that Mom was pretty overwhelmed, as well. I was the oldest; and since there were always younger siblings requiring Mom's attention, when I wasn't helping with them, I was pretty much on my own.

There were hardly any children in our neighborhood, so I spent most of my time by myself watching our old black and white TV, reading or simply daydreaming. Dad wasn't around to teach me how to throw a baseball or to do many of the things boys should learn to do. I'm not blaming him. His childhood was a literal nightmare, growing up during the war years with his mom working fulltime in a defense plant and his dad needing long-term medical care in a hospital somewhere.

Bullies Have a Kind of Radar

When I started school, I was the youngest and one of the smallest boys in my class. You would have thought that I had a bullseye on my forehead that drew every bully in school. Bullies have a kind of radar - a wimp-seeking guidance system that enables them to zero in on the weakest kids around. The fact that I didn't know anything about sports or guy stuff didn't help either.

When reflecting on my experience in Catholic grade school I often comment that it rained every day. I imagine that's an exaggeration, but that's actually how it felt. In addition to not playing sports and getting picked on by the numerous bullies in my school, I didn't do well with my grades either. Every lousy report card I brought home, which was most of them, always elicited the same stream of negative comments from Dad. "Why can't you be like everybody else?" "You're so stupid!" "You'll never amount to anything!" These platitudes never motivated me to improve. They only seemed to cement the negative image I had of myself.

Beginning to See Myself in a Different Light

Things began to change for me after joining Boy Scouts. Our Scoutmaster was Sam. He was a tough Korean War veteran and knew how to inspire young men. Under his leadership, I began to see myself in a different light. I enjoyed the praise Sam and others gave me as I accomplished goals, mastered new skills and moved up in rank. I eventually became an Eagle Scout before finally hanging up my Scout uniform my freshman year in high school.

Also in high school, I stood up to my first bully. He was beating up on one of my younger brothers. He was much stronger than me and certainly much more experienced in schoolyard brawls than I was. I couldn't take it anymore. I called him out to stop picking on my kid brother so he came after me. I lost the fight badly. The funny thing was that after that all those bullies left me alone. I guess they decided that it wasn't worth it if I was going to fight back. I later discovered that bullies are really cowards who prey on the weakest among us. They usually don't have the stomach for a real fight.

I was in high school in the early seventies, during the Vietnam War. There was great social unrest at that time and the drug culture was invading our public school. Some of my friends were experimenting with illegal drugs and invited me to join them. I had other friends who were thinking about going out for the football team. I chose to hang out with the athletically inclined, even though I wasn't very athletic myself, yet. This one choice has made a huge difference in my life.

Ability Without Character Is Not Enough

I was still small for my age and pretty inexperienced in sports when I first went out for football, so I sat on the bench most of my sophomore and junior years. At the football banquet my junior year, when most of my classmates were getting their varsity letters and I didn't, something rose up inside me, a steeled determination to never miss out on this again. In that moment I committed to work as hard as I could to be in the best physical condition possible and to be the finest football player I could be.

I lived in the weight room and initiated a rigorous exercise and agility program. Ultimately, the results were more than I had hoped for. My overall body weight went from 145 pounds to 175 pounds, and I became one of the fastest players on the team. That year I learned the value of setting goals and hard work. But I also learned that ability without character was not enough.

I observed certain members of our team that were bullies like the ones I dealt with growing up. Everything seemed to come easy to them; that was, until the chips were down. When a bully or coward is confronted by a stressful situation, and there are plenty of these during a competitive football game, they have no deep reservoir of inner strength to draw upon. When we face struggles, we often need to draw from something deep inside ourselves to persevere. I call that character, and since bullies have none they usually fold up like a house of cards.

I discovered that as I achieved my goals in athletics my self-esteem along with my grades and personal relationships improved.

A Band of Brothers

I also learned that the sum of the parts of a team of average players that were united as a true "band of brothers" was greater than a few "stars". During my senior year of high school football, I saw firsthand how a band of brothers will almost always overcome a loosely knit team of stars.

I loved playing on that football team. We were part of something special and we knew it. Only one of us went on to play college football on a scholarship. As players we were pretty average, but we had heart and were determined never to give up. Most of the teams we faced that year were far more talented than we were, but we lost only one game that season.

In fact, our cross-town rival won almost every game by thirty points. They had many talented players, including a running back with over a ten-yard per carry average. Hardly anyone in town expected us to beat them except our coaches and ourselves. I remember telling some of my classmates that we really believed we would win the big game that Thanksgiving. It was wonderful running onto the field that day and seeing a huge sign painted over the stands with the words, "We Believe".

One of my cherished memories was that of hearing the crowd chanting, "We believe, we believe" over and over again as the clock ran down on our 7-0 win that day! I didn't realize until many years later how important that lesson in "believing" would be in my life.

Doesn't God Care?

One day I was speaking with my stepbrother who was studying to become a priest. I liked messing with people by telling them that God is either dead or there is no God at all. I knew that there was no such thing as an atheist. I, like so many others, was angry with God. If there's a "big man upstairs", isn't He big enough to help relieve some of the suffering down here? Doesn't He care? In my frustration I used to say that if there is a God, He would have to be perfect. Since His creation is so *im*perfect with sickness, wars and disasters rampant all over the world, either there can't be a God, He doesn't care or He's dead.

My stepbrother suggested a different possibility for me to think about regarding the nature of God and the world. What he told me was something I had never considered before. It was, however, the genesis of a train of thought that eventually caused the image of God that I had created in my mind to come crashing down around me.

The idea my stepbrother planted in my mind was both simple and profound - maybe God made the world perfect, gave us free will, and we messed it all up! That was a turning point for me because it showed that God was personally involved in the world and that He proved His love for us by giving us this beautiful planet. It also began to answer for me the question as to how evil entered God's creation. This line of reasoning didn't answer all of my questions, but it enabled me to get over my anger with God and actually drove me to seek Him for answers.

The Night Everything Changed

One late summer evening everything changed for me. I had turned twenty-five years of age about a month before, and I had been looking for answers for some time. Walking into the meeting hall I was wondering how I came to this point. I was a professed atheist, a workaholic who hardly had time to sleep; and here I was coming to this place to spend a whole evening with people I hardly knew, listening to some speaker from the Midwest that I didn't know either. What was I thinking? This is how I got there....

I had become quite ill over the previous year. I had been to a number of doctors, including a specialist. No one could figure out what was wrong with me. I was a fairly successful sales rep for a hardware distributor, and my territory was in southern New England. It was a beautiful place to live, especially in the fall, but I really didn't appreciate it at the time. I was far too busy working night and day, seven days a week, to notice. This fast-paced lifestyle and my around-the-clock work habits eventually took its toll on me, and I began having episodes of pretty severe physical symptoms from some unknown illness. These symptoms included my heart beating rapidly and palpitating, breaking out in a cold sweat, and shallow breathing, accompanied at times by dizziness. It got so bad earlier that summer that I could hardly drive to my customers' stores. Today I know that they were panic attacks, brought on by high levels of work-related stress. At that time, however, no one I knew had the expertise or experience to make that diagnosis.

On one particularly bad day while I was still hours from home, I began suffering frequent episodes of severe panic attacks. These were only exasperated by the heat and humidity of the day, especially since my company car was not air-conditioned at the time. To make matters even worse, the radio announcer kept reminding me over and over again that the temperature was a steamy 102 degrees. He kept repeating this witty play on words because the radio station I was tuned to was 102.9 FM. I used to listen to that station back then because they had a nice mix of oldies and current hits. That day, however, the constant reminders of the 102-degree temperature didn't help my state of mind or my symptoms. You would think that I would have had the presence of mind to change the station, but in that part of New England there weren't a lot of other options. All things considered, though, it probably would have been worse turning the radio off. If I was left alone with my thoughts, I would likely have felt even more stress. At least the radio was somewhat of a distraction from my symptoms.

It took me a very long time to make it home that day, having to stop along the way to cool down and catch my breath. Finally, after arriving home hours later than normal, I poured myself a cold drink and went downstairs where it was cooler. I collapsed into my easy chair exhausted from the day and found myself saying these words, "God, there's got to be more to life than this!" I just didn't understand why this was happening to me. I had everything the world told me should make me happy, money, relationships, cars and more. Why was I so miserable? Why was I in such physical and emotional turmoil?

"God, There's Got to Be More to Life Than This!"

At the moment that I said those few simple words, "God, there's got to be more to life than this", I felt something change on the inside of me, down deep in my belly. It was almost imperceptible, but I felt like something clicked inside, knowing at the same time that everything would be all right. Ironically, I had completely missed the fact that this day was also my birthday. Little did I know how appropriate that was because the events of that day, my 25th birthday, would alter the course of the rest of my life.

About the same time that all this was happening, my company opened a new account with one of the largest retailers in my area, and we became one of their hardware suppliers. Although they had agreed to use us, they were slow getting started. I decided to spend more time there hoping to get things moving. This gave me the unexpected opportunity to become acquainted with the store manager. He was a really nice guy and very knowledgeable about our industry, and he appeared to have taken a liking to me.

I found that the manager was not only passionate about work but that he had other interests, as well. Some of them went much deeper than running a store or a company. I wasn't really sure what these interests were all about at the time, but I was intrigued by the fact that he knew something about life that I didn't. He eventually invited me to come to a meeting at the offices of a local manufacturer to hear a speaker from Chicago who was also his mentor. This speaker was a retired aeronautical engineer who had become a pastor. I was told that the speaker was scheduled to speak on various topics related to the spiritual side of life. I felt in my heart that I should go; and since my life was falling apart anyway, what would it hurt?

I decided to go hear this speaker from Chicago, but I didn't want to go alone. I invited my wife and my mom, and the three of us joined the store manager and his friend at the event. I can't recall what the pastor's topic was that evening, but I do remember quite vividly what happened there.

Healed in a Flash

 The five of us were sitting in the back row of the meeting hall. It was a nice facility that could seat a few hundred people comfortably. About halfway through the pastor's talk I began to have the symptoms of a severe panic attack. Not wanting to embarrass my host or myself I stood up to leave. Beginning to move down the aisle I happened to look up at the speaker who was teaching at the front of the room. Suddenly I saw a bright white light completely encircle him, and then I saw him bow his head. The next thing that happened was truly amazing. As soon as he dropped his head a bolt of brilliant light shot down from the front of the room and hit me. That lightning strike was so strong that it literally threw me back into my chair. This flash of electricity surged through my entire body and then slowly dissipated. I sat there dazed, wondering what had happened. It was then I realized that all my symptoms had disappeared. I was completely healed from the panic attacks that had plagued me for years, and I have been free from them ever since.

After the message concluded I overheard my mom mention that she felt the surge of energy I had experienced. Someone else asked excitedly, "Did you see the light around the pastor?" It was nice to hear these confirmations, but I knew even without them that something really significant happened to me that night - that God was way more than just "the man upstairs". I had never experienced that kind of power before. It was awe-inspiring, life-changing and good all at the same time. All I thought I knew about God and the world was gone in a flash, literally!

Freedom from Fear

One of the additional things I noticed after I was touched by God's healing light was that not only was I healed from the symptoms of severe panic attacks but I was also delivered from the cause of the disease, which is fear. In that momentary flash of light, the manifested healing presence of God literally evaporated all of my fears.

My physical and emotional healing were a gift of God's love for me. I knew then that God loved me just the way I was and His perfect love drove out all my fears. If the Creator of the universe is on our side who is there to fear anyway? My emotional healing was almost as beneficial as my physical healing because the peace of mind that comes from being free from fear is priceless.

I can't say that I have remained totally free from all fear whatsoever. I *can* say that when fear tries to return, I refocus my mind from the thoughts that are causing my fearful emotions to thinking about God, His protection and blessings. In a short time, all my fears dissipate.

After encountering God's presence in that flash of light I also realized that there was more to this life than what meets the eye. After that experience I knew that there was an intelligent, benevolent power at work in this world that was beyond what I had learned at home, in church or in school. More than anything else I wanted to learn more about what happened to me that night. I hadn't read a book since graduating from college, but I began reading anything I could get my hands on that might possibly give me a clue to who or what I just encountered. I had been touched by a spiritual reality that showed me "Someone" very powerful not only existed but cared for me. This brought significance and meaning to my life, and I wanted more.

When I was struck by God's healing power that evening I was not only thrown back into my chair, but I was thrown into a whole new direction in life. I was thrown into a place of knowing that no matter what anyone says to the contrary, God still heals today. I was thrown into an understanding that not only is there an unseen hand at work in the universe but that He is personal and cares about each of us. I was thrown into a state of questioning everything I knew or believed and everyone I had ever heard. I was thrown into a quest to *know* the God I encountered that fateful day.

Another side effect of encountering this divine light (which I later discovered was actually the presence of God and His life) was that my relationship with some of my friends and family changed. You see, not everyone is ready for or desires the personal reality of God's presence. Some are drawn to His light while others still cling to the darkness. It can be difficult for us at times as friends and family pull away from us, sensing that something is "different" about us. The silver lining is that the relationships we gain with others who are drawn to God can bring us incredible joy and happiness, not just here but for eternity.

It is important to note that God's transformative light doesn't have to come in a flash but can grow within a person gradually, which is more common. It's important to mention, too, that I didn't ask for any of this to happen. I wasn't looking for God specifically that evening, but I was seeking answers and was stepping out of my comfort zone. Our part is to seek, ask and to be open. That's really it. God is the one responsible for the answers. He knows us better than we know ourselves, and we just need to trust that He has our best interest in mind. It is up to God to decide how and when He reveals Himself.

As I mentioned before I wasn't really seeking God when He found me, just answers and relief from my physical symptoms. However, now that I have found Him, a big part of my journey in life is to seek more of the light of His presence. Once you've had an encounter with God you can never have enough. It's like having a complete abiding sense of having it all, while at the same time wanting to experience more and more but never totally getting it all. It's awesome!

I have been asked numerous times over the years to share some of my journey with others. I feel now that the time is right to do that. I hope that you find this helpful as you contemplate and walk the path set before you. My hope for you is that you encounter the light of God's presence, as well; whether it is in a flash of lightening that changes everything in a moment, or in the gradual dawning of a new day that transforms your life little by little for the better. Just remember that not only is God the source of the light, He *is* the Light. As a wise author once wrote, *"Walk in the light as He is in the light." (1 John 1:7)*

The Rest of the Story

The rest of this book is about my journey with God, the experiences I had along the way and the lessons I learned from them. I hope they inspire you as they have me to always want to see more of God's life manifesting through us all, thus making a difference for His Kingdom in this world.

2. MAN MADE GOD IN HIS IMAGE

God Saved My Life

It was a damp, foggy day. I was late for a meeting, so I was driving on Route 50 near Chicago too fast for conditions. Out of the fog a stop sign appeared suddenly at an intersection, and there were cars crossing my path right in front of me. I slammed on the brakes trying to stop, but there wasn't enough time. My car began to spin out of control. Just then I had an amazing peace come over me, and I had the unusual sensation of being more aware of the spirit than my body while still holding the steering wheel.

I had the awareness that God was right there with no separation between us. My body was just a vehicle much like my car, and the real me was totally aware of everything going on around me and the presence of God at the same time. No fear, anxiousness, or worry intruded; just peace and timelessness. One of the weirdest sensations I had was that everything slowed down to almost a standstill. As my car spun close to one of the other vehicles in the intersection I just said, "Can't hit that one", and my car spun and missed it. As I spun into the next lane I was approached by another car in the intersection and said, "Can't hit that one"; and once again my car spun away missing it.

As my car kept spinning it eventually spun into the roadside drainage ditch and started to approach a metal fence. Still in the spirit I said, "Can't hit the fence", and instantly my vehicle shuddered to a stop. The engine had died while my car was spinning; but I turned the key, the engine roared back to life, and I drove up out of the ditch and headed to my meeting. I was very thankful for God's intervention and much wiser about driving on wet, foggy days.

I believe that if God were just like us, He wouldn't have been able to intervene in my near accident that day. I cringe when thinking about what *could* have happened to me and the other people in that intersection if He hadn't intervened. I have thought about that day many times over the years. My two young boys might have had to grow up without a dad. What would have happened to the others if this had gone a different way? How much pain and suffering that one mistake could have caused! I am so grateful for God's mercy and protection. He can make all the difference in our lives. I will return to this story and another one like it in the next chapter.

If this incident had happened just a few years earlier when I was questioning God, His motives and even His existence, the outcome might have been very different. I'd like to share with you some of that journey.

What Is Your Understanding About God?

Over the years I have asked a simple question of countless numbers of people in small group settings and in one-on-one sessions. I usually begin a small discussion group or a counseling session with this question because the answer I get gives me a pretty accurate indicator of how I need to proceed. The question I usually ask is, "What is your understanding about God?"

As you can imagine I receive many different answers to this

question. The way someone responds determines how we begin our conversation. Their answer usually uncovers some misunderstanding about the true nature of God. This is significant because it is almost always our perception of God and His motives that holds us back from enjoying more meaning and contentment in life.

I have learned that everyone has a philosophy of life - a view of the world that we live by that informs our decisions and governs our behavior. If someone says that they have no philosophy of life, well, that's actually a philosophy! A person's worldview is their own, and they are welcome to live by it as long as their behavior doesn't impinge on the rights of others. However, not all philosophies of life are equal because they don't all produce optimum health, wealth and wellbeing.

I believe that a worldview that originates with the Creator of humanity and the world will be the most effective in realizing an optimum life. Almost everyone is looking for their purpose in life and for why they are here. However, the only person qualified to answer these questions is our Designer.

Woody Allen Finds a VW

I was thinking about the importance of finding our purpose and was reminded about a clip from a movie I saw years ago called *Sleeper*. In this movie the main character, played by Woody Allen, lives in the distant future where cars are no longer used and somehow stumbles upon an ancient Volkswagen Beetle.

Now let's imagine if this character had no idea how the designer intended to use this piece of metal. If there was still enough juice in the battery to play the entertainment center, he might think the car was a sound booth. If he noticed that the seats reclined, he might speculate that the VW was for camping. If he finally fired up the engine and somehow put it in gear, he might discover that the car was designed to take someone from point A to point B.

The highest and best use for a product is determined by its inventor. In our example, the automobile was designed to move us from one place to another; in a word, transportation. As I mentioned, if someone isn't familiar with the best use of an automobile, they might mistakenly believe that a car is made for some other purpose. I understand that this is a pretty simple metaphor, but you get the idea that only the creator of something or someone can really define its purpose and give it its meaning.

True Wealth Is Living Out Our Purpose in Life

In my view, the foundation of an effective philosophy is one that acknowledges God as our Creator because only our inventor can reveal to us our purpose - <u>why</u> we were created. Additionally, our perception of God and His nature are also contributing factors in the effectiveness of our worldview and our capacity to experience a fulfilling and satisfying life.

I have found that true wealth is an important part of a fulfilling life. Many people and families experience stress in their lives due to financial issues. However, I don't advocate the seeking of money as a reason for living. I believe that if we seek the purpose for which we were created, the true wealth that we need will follow. When our purpose becomes our work, then we will be making a living doing what we love.

Please don't be turned off because of my use of the word "wealth". I know that there has been a lot of misuse in certain circles regarding wealth and prosperity. However, this is not what I mean by true wealth. Just having money does not necessarily mean that someone is truly wealthy.

For example, becoming a millionaire does not guarantee that a person will be content. According to a recent study most millionaires felt as if they were living on a treadmill and felt that they had sacrificed their families in pursuit of financial gain. (<u>UBS Investor Watch</u> 2Q 2015, "When is enough, enough, Why the wealthy can't get off the treadmill") I believe that this points to the reality that money without contentment is not true wealth.

A very wise man once wrote to one of his students named Timothy, *"A godly life brings huge profits to people who are content with what they have. We didn't bring anything into the world, and we can't take anything out of it." (1 Timothy 6:6 – 7 GW)*

Therefore, I contend that true wealth is living the life God intended us to live. It's not only important to have the health and the financial wherewithal needed to fulfill our purpose. We also need to be at peace with where we are in our journey. This for me is the definition of health, wealth, and wellbeing or contentment.

The Man Upstairs

Sometimes when I ask people, "What is your understanding about God?" they will refer to God as "the man upstairs" or compare Him to someone they knew in the past like a parent or teacher. This at least shows that they believe there is a God and that He is aware of what is happening to them and could help them if He wants to.

The inherent weakness in this perception about God is that He is sort of "like us". Even though He is immortal, all-knowing, and all powerful, this perception of God is that He still thinks and acts like us. This means that we are left with a God of our own creation. I have heard it said many times that we are made in God's image. However, I have discovered most people's perception of God is that He is made more in our image rather than the other way around, which is the reality. Any concept of God that is created by a human being will be quite flawed - how could a creature define a limitless Creator? A God made in our image would not be much help in a crisis, now would He?

There's an interesting line that Bill Murray gives in the movie *Groundhog Day* that demonstrates this limited perception about God when he says, "Maybe God isn't omnipotent. He's just been around so long He knows everything." This view of God may seem harmless on the surface, but it is very limiting because it leads us to attribute human characteristics to God. Just look at the Roman and Greek pantheons of gods. They were basically larger, more powerful versions of human beings and were as prone to the same weaknesses and passions as were their human creators. Aren't we doing the same thing when we think of God as being like us? How can we trust God to carry us through the most difficult and challenging situations in life if He is not much more than a larger version of ourselves?

I have learned that thinking of God as if He had human characteristics is not only limiting but cannot be further from the truth. As one of the wisest men who ever lived, the prophet Isaiah, wrote about God under divine inspiration, *"For My thoughts are not your thoughts, nor are your ways My ways," says the Lord. "For as the heavens are higher than the earth, so are My ways higher than your ways, and My thoughts than your thoughts." (Isaiah 55:8-9 NKJV)*

Now this is a God that we can trust to find answers in those situations in life that appear to have no possible solution. A God whose thoughts and ways are higher than the heavens are above the earth can carry us through anything we might face, even death. This is also the only kind of God that is worthy of worship. Did you know that even the word "worship" comes from the old English word "worth"? We worship God because He alone is worth it!

I believe that when we attribute human characteristics to God, we are actually making God in our image, which is actually the exact opposite of reality. Therefore, the God we create will be our own invention drawn from our personal experiences and expectations. If our parents were cold and unloving that may very well be how we see God. If our experience with religion or religious people was that they were self-righteous and judgmental, then we may look at God in that way.

I have found that many people also see God as a strict disciplinarian and a real joy-killer. They see Him as "up there somewhere" waiting for us to step out of line and then smack us down. There is a real coldness attributed to a God that comes from this perception. They will imply that God is all about the rules, and if you want to keep Him on your side you better not break them. It's really hard to love and be loved with this point of view.

We've all known people over the years that are good at pointing out our faults. Many see God as the supreme fault-finder, always seeing us through our mistakes and weaknesses. People who believe that God sees them this way tend to be very critical of others, as well. In my experience, fault-finders are very cold and unloving people because fault-finding is the opposite of love. Love is blind to imperfections and faults!

I have observed that when people see God as a fault-finder they often struggle with trust and the ability to display love to others. This is because they don't feel the love and acceptance of God; therefore, they tend to be quite judgmental of other people. Love is about accepting someone just as they are.

When we open ourselves to consider the possibility that God loves us not because of what we've done but because of who He is and that we are His kids, we begin to come to a very different conclusion about His character. This changes our relationship with

Him because we know He love us unconditionally and wants the best for us. This revelation of His love for us and that He accepts us just the way we are enables us to fall in love with Him, which fills our hearts with heavenly joy and peace. That's exactly what happened to me.

Our journey in life is not to find "the man upstairs" or the God of "our creation". It is to discover that God has been with us all along. He cares for us and wants to have an intimate relationship with us. "Finding" God is about growing in a relationship with a Person who is the journey *and* the destination. Jesus of Nazareth said it best when He said, *"I am the way, the truth, and the life."*

As long as I can remember I felt like something big, really big was coming but I didn't know what it was…

3. WE ALL NEED TO BE PART OF SOMETHING BIG

Most of my life leading up to my first supernatural encounter with God I felt such a need to fit in, to be part of the in crowd, to be accepted by my peers, but I never was. I don't know if that's your experience, too, but I have talked to many people who have felt that way.

Much of that changed for me after I was touched by the healing power of God. Once I experienced that God was real and personal, I began to become more and more aware of His abiding presence. This reminded me of the feeling you get when you are outside on a sunny spring day. I literally felt clean on the *inside*, like you feel after a shower. I could also feel the subtle weight and warmth of His constant embrace upon me as if sunshine could feel heavy and warm on your skin. In addition, I had a peace and contentment that is almost impossible to describe.

I felt so blessed, favored and grateful. I knew that whatever I asked for He would give. The funny thing was that all I wanted was to abide in Him and Him in me. However, when I did ask God for something, such as healing for someone or help with a problem, it was always answered. This was the first time in my life that I felt like I belonged and was accepted and loved unconditionally. When you know that you know the Creator of the universe loves you, nothing else matters.

This awareness of God's presence stayed with me for many months. It began to fade, though, as the cares and distractions of life crowded it out. I have learned that when I pray and seek Him, His presence returns in a very tangible way, which has been intensifying over the years. I believe that this experience is available to everyone. We just need to believe, seek and expect.

I believe that there is an inherent need that we all have to be part of something far greater than ourselves. This comes from the fact that we were created to live in and to contain God. This reminds me of a popular quote that is attributed to the famous French mathematician and philosopher, Blaise Pascal, who is quoted as saying, "There is a God-shaped vacuum in the heart of every man which cannot be filled by any created thing, but only by God the Creator, made known through Jesus Christ."

The Apostle Paul, who wrote a significant portion of the Biblical New Testament, said something very similar as he was explaining about the one true God to the Greek philosophers at Mars Hill in Athens when he said, *"for in Him we live and move and have our being, as also some of your own poets have said, 'For we are also His offspring.'"* (*Acts 17:28*) To live and move and have our very being (nature, identity, and value) in an intimate relationship with the Creator and source of everything is really, really big! Now that much of humanity has lost the awareness of God's presence and love, people wander about the world looking for something big enough to fill their emptiness and to satisfy the lack of meaning in their lives.

Time Stood Still

Playing football in high school and later in college certainly did enable me to enjoy a greater sense of purpose and meaning than any other endeavor I had been involved in up to that time. Something quite unique happened to me during a football game my senior year in high school that showed me there was a power at work in the world (and in my life) that was far greater than I had ever imagined.

It happened during the fourth game of my senior season. It was the last play of the first half. Our team had not been scored on in the first 3-1/2 games of the year. The opposing team was on our one-yard line. There was only enough time left in the half for one more play. I was playing defensive tackle on the right side of the ball. My intention at the time was to do my part to stop them from scoring, so when the ball was hiked, I dove forward. Unfortunately, the ball carrier ran to the other side of the field away from me. Even though it was physically impossible for me to stop him from scoring from where I was, I followed my intention and pursued him along the goal line. As I moved in the direction of the guy with the ball the strangest thing happened. Everyone except me went into slow motion. I was the only one on the field who could move with any speed, so I ran over and tackled him on the one-yard line. Then, just as suddenly, everyone else's rate of movement went back to normal, the half ended and our shutout string was saved. I recall sitting in the locker room during halftime feeling an indescribable sense of peace and wonder. I didn't know how or what happened - only that it was way bigger than anything I had experienced before!

In that moment I learned that there was much more to life than meets the eye. I also discovered that there are dimensions of time and space that are beyond our five senses. I had a similar experience years later while I was in a car that was spinning out of control.

Some of you reading this are probably thinking that this is nuts, that these things don't happen, or this can't be God. Sorry, but this really did happen, just this way. I am alive today because God did intervene in a very similar way when my car was out of control, and I've been able to help others over the years because God has brought me safely through those situations. God didn't cause these problems to happen; but He was always there to help me through the various crises in life, even those caused by my weaknesses and foolish mistakes.

The first time everything around me slowed down I was on the football field and not aware of God's presence; but the second time, in my car, I was. I've heard many people try to describe the sensation of everything slowing down in a car accident or in some other crisis. It's difficult to describe. It's as if the separation between the spirit and the physical becomes very thin at these times. Being strangely separate from my body watching those events unfold around me, my car spinning out of control, just missing other vehicles and barriers, and calmly speaking with God about what needed to happen was quite an experience. It was only because of the fact that my Heavenly Father responded to my requests that I emerged from that event unscathed and without causing any injury or property damage. I'm glad that these events happened because they remind me that there's a lot more to life than meets the eye.

Events like these can help emphasize the importance of focus in our lives. As we learn to focus intently on our deepest purpose, basically our *"one thing"*, we will be much more likely to accomplish our deepest goals and desires in spite of any obstacles we may encounter. (One of the lessons I learned from this was that focusing on our purpose, the *why* we are here, is a far deeper motivation than just setting goals.) Discovering our purpose is a key step in finding meaning and satisfaction in life. Then, if we fervently focus on the "Source" of that purpose we will not only be empowered to achieve our goals and aspirations but will also see our lives being transformed over time by our growing relationship with that Source. The journey to discover our purpose in life is also a quest for the revelation of God, and in the process, becoming the person that we've always wished we could be.

We are transformed because we become like the people we spend the most time with. As Charlie Tremendous Jones once said, "You will be the same person in five years as you are today except for the people you meet and the books you read." Imagine what we will be like in five years if we spend that time focused on the Person who knows our purpose better than anyone else, God.

Recently, while focusing on my current revelation of God's purpose for my life, the memory of that football play where time stood still came flooding back. At that moment I realized that one reason I was given that experience on the football field might have been to show me that no situation is impossible for God. I also learned that by focusing on God's deep purpose for my life and how His life and influence can help others, the miraculous power of God would become more commonplace in my daily experience.

We Should Expect Miracles

There are many miracles recorded in the Bible, such as Jesus escaping through a crowd, walking on water, or His feeding over 5,000 people with a few loaves and fishes. God is a big God, and the works He did in the past He's still doing today. I know that God wants life on earth to be just like it is in heaven. When we see a situation here on earth that is contrary to what life would be in heaven, such as sickness, poverty, hate, crime, and other things, we pray that these issues get in line with God's will and become consistent with the way things are in heaven. We call this a miracle, but it's actually the way life should be here on earth as long as everything in this world is coherent with God's desires. That's why Jesus prayed, *"Your (God's) Kingdom come Your will be done on earth as it is in heaven." (Matthew 6: 10)*

I'm living proof that God still does miracles because He cured me of a debilitating illness that the doctors couldn't help me with. I also know there are millions more around the world like me. I'm hoping that these stories will raise your expectation that God can still work miracles in your life. Since I know He loves me and I know He also loves you, He has the miracle you need waiting for you.

We were made by God to have dominion in the earth. As Moses wrote, *"Then God said, 'Let Us make man in Our image, according to Our likeness; let them have dominion… over all the earth…'" (Genesis 1: 26)* We are supposed to rule over this world as His representatives and subdue anything that opposes God's will. Therefore, the struggle to compete in a sporting event can be very fulfilling because I believe that it has a way of touching us at our very core. Struggling against an opponent or experiencing God's protection or provision in a crisis situation is reminiscent of one of the main reasons we exist.

I believe that one of the reasons we are here is for His pleasure. *"You are worthy, O Lord, to receive glory, honor and power: for You have created all things, and for Your pleasure they are and were created." (Revelations 4:11 KJV)*

I contend that God takes pleasure in seeing us overcome evil in our lives and in this world through the power of Jesus' name, by faith in His name, as the Apostle Luke reported regarding the Apostle Peter did when healing a man who had been crippled for 40 years.

"His name, through faith in His name, has made this man strong." (Acts 3:16a)

We desire to be part of something bigger than ourselves because we instinctively know that we were designed for so much more than merely surviving from paycheck to paycheck or from day to day. We were created by God so that God could rule this world through us. What could be bigger than that?

Don't Live from the Sidelines

As I'm writing this, I am thinking of a comment someone made to me about sports years ago. "What is a sporting event? It's a handful of very fit individuals exercising in front of thousands of people in dire need of exercise."

There is a valuable lesson here in that a life best lived is not one from the sidelines but by being in the game. To be truly fulfilled we need to find out our purpose in life so that we can actually be who we were created to be and do what we were designed to do. If we know who we are, then what we do will flow out of that. One of the best questions I ever asked myself was, "What would I do for a living if money were no object?"

Most of us let other people and circumstances set our direction in life. Rather than seeking our Creator for direction in what we should be and do in life, we usually just fall into a job or career. Most of us let life happen to us. The good news is that it's never too late to change! If we start moving in the direction for which we were created we will find much more fulfillment and meaning in what we do, and the money will follow.

When I reminisce about playing sports back in school a line from a song by Big Joe Shelton comes to mind, "The older I get the better I was." It's pretty funny, but there's also a kernel of truth when you really think about it.

I remember sharing stories with my brothers-in-law about our high school football exploits almost every time we'd get together. It was a lot of fun, and I felt as if it were just yesterday, even though many years had passed. Speaking about these shared experiences made me feel like I was still part of something bigger than myself. Reminiscing about being part of a team, how we helped each other overcome an adversary and achieve something special fills a deep longing in our souls. It's too bad these experiences don't last. I suppose this is the case because they were never designed to be the focus in life anyway. They are just sign posts along the journey. They do, however, remind us that we are looking for something that could give our lives meaning and purpose. Neither sporting events nor their memories can satisfy our emptiness for very long. The risk in trying to hold onto them is that we might miss something even bigger and more satisfying.

I believe that we are drawn to these memories because we were designed to play a part in a huge story that is unfolding all around us. We are mostly unaware of this story; but when larger-than-life experiences come our way such as sporting events, movies, reunions, and celebrations we sometimes get an inkling of that hidden reality that is so much larger than ordinary life.

Looking for Love in So Many Faces

Country singer Jonny Lee's hit song *"Looking for Love"* struck a similar note about the search for love and meaning in life. The words of the song show a deep need for our heart to be filled with love. The song goes on to say that we "are looking for love in all the wrong places, looking for love in so many faces". This shows that human beings are searching for a love to fill the God-sized hole in our hearts. The only love that can fill this longing is the infinite, unconditional love of our Creator. Since we don't realize that He is the only one who can fill our emptiness we look to the love of other people and the things of this world to fill that void.

We turn to the trappings of the world, such as the affections of others, our jobs, alcohol and drugs, entertainment, and sports; but nothing seems to work.

Deep down we all need to be part of something bigger than ourselves. That's one reason why whole cities and countries identify with their local or national sporting events. When our team wins, we all cheer as if we were there playing alongside the team members.

Sports can be a very good thing, not just for exercise but also for what it can teach us about getting along with others, the value of hard work and how to set and achieve goals. I know in my life being part of a team taught me very valuable lessons: perseverance, patience and collaboration. However, sports or anything else that we use as a replacement for God will eventually become unbalanced and consume us as we let it become an idol in our life.

Living a Life of Great Value

I contend that we all have a primary purpose here on earth, which is for God to dwell in our hearts by the Holy Spirit and to let Him live His life through us. If this is all we ever discover about our unique purpose and design we have lived a life of great value. However, if we learn what God has created us specifically to do in this world, we can find amazing joy and satisfaction here on earth and later in eternity. Our understanding of the purpose God has for our lives will likely grow as our relationship with Him and our ability to hear His voice deepens. We often feel like we are seeing our purpose change; but what is really happening is that we are realizing the scope of our purpose in greater and greater measure, which creates even more meaning for us.

This personal transformation is brought about by knowing that

God is with us, that He's big enough to handle anything that comes our way, and that He has promised to be an ever-present help in trouble. This produces a confidence in that we know we can always count on Him. Many people don't know that they can trust God no matter what. I have discovered that God can be trusted to fulfill His promises. He has always shown Himself to be faithful, even in life-and-death situations, in my own life and the lives of others. This gives me a peace and joy that is beyond words, no matter what comes my way. I take comfort in what King David wrote, "God is our refuge and strength, A very present help in trouble." (Psalm 46:1)

"When I Run, I Feel His Pleasure"

One of my favorite movies is *Chariots of Fire,* which won the Academy Award for Best Picture in 1984. The plot of the movie is drawn from a comparison of the lives of two Olympic runners and their different approaches to finding meaning and purpose in life through athletics during the 1924 Olympic Games.

Harold Abrahams was likely the fastest sprinter in England at the time, and until the Olympic trials he had never lost a race. The movie depicts Harold as having a very tortured soul due to the persecution he had received over the years for being Jewish. Harold is asked in the movie, "Do you love running?" He answers, "It is more of a compulsion, a weapon ... against being Jewish, I suppose".

The reason Harold was running in competition wasn't because he loved fulfilling his purpose. It was to help fill the emptiness he felt inside. Running for Harold became more of a drug than a meaningful endeavor in life. Human glory and fame can, like drugs, satisfy our emptiness for a while; but we eventually need more and more to be satisfied. Harold's moment of truth happened when he raced Eric Liddell, a Scottish rugby player and missionary to China.

Eric and Harold competed in the 100-yard dash at a qualifying meet prior to the Olympic Games. To everyone's surprise, Eric soundly defeated Harold in that race. There's a great scene where Harold is sitting in the empty grandstands after he lost the race, looking as if he had just lost his best friend; and in the background you hear the maintenance crew folding up the bleacher chairs one at a time, sounding like nails being driven into the lid of a coffin.

Harold was feeling like his life was over. He found that his reason for living was based on something that doesn't last and can't fully satisfy. It is so important that we find the purpose that we were uniquely created to fulfill and to pursue it with a motivation that lasts beyond this life.

Harold went on to acquire a mentor who helped him compete at a higher level in the Olympic Games. This coach made a huge difference in his performance. He won the gold medal for the 100-yard dash in the 1924 Olympics and for a brief time Harold was crowned the fastest man in the world.

Harold possessed many gifts. He was an accomplished musician, vocalist and stage performer. He was also accepted at the finest university in the land and was a superior athlete. I believe the main weakness that kept Harold from realizing true satisfaction and joy from his accomplishments was that he had the wrong reason for trying to achieve in the first place.

The things we do and our accomplishments in life can leave us feeling empty and unfulfilled if they are not designed with our "one thing" in mind. If we are to be truly fulfilled over the course of our entire lives, our "one thing" needs to be of lasting value. Harold believed that winning an Olympic gold medal would give his life the meaning and purpose he craved. What he didn't realize was how short-lived the feeling of fulfillment would be, even when winning one of the greatest of these events.

If we live our lives knowing that God dwells in us and He is doing our tasks through us, then we will always feel valued and everything we do will be meaningful.

Now let's contrast Harold's purpose and motivation with that of Eric Liddell's. There is a scene in the movie where the future king of Great Britain and the rest of the Olympic Committee are trying to get Eric to run in the qualifying heat for the 100-yard dash, which happened to be on a Sunday. Eric refused to run because he believed that Sundays were set aside to worship God, and he felt that competing on that day would be wrong. Because of his stand, Eric was going to be disqualified from the race. I really respect Eric's courage in standing up for his convictions in the face of some very powerful opposition.

One of Eric's teammates saved the day by offering Eric to take his place in the quarter-mile event instead of the 100-yard dash. During this scene one of the committee members, Lord Birkenhead, tells another member, the Duke of Sutherland, "Thank God for Lindsay (Eric's teammate). I thought the lad (Liddell) had us beaten." The Duke of Southerland replies, "He did have us beaten, and thank God he did." Then Lord Birkenhead says, "I don't quite follow you". The Duke of Southerland replies, "The 'lad', as you call him, is a true man of principles and a true athlete. His speed is a mere extension of his life, its force. We sought to sever his running from himself."

Eric went on to win the gold medal for the quarter mile, an almost impossible feat given that he had had two qualifying heats that day. Here is a wonderful quote of Eric Liddell's from the movie: "I believe God made me for a purpose, but he also made me fast! And when I run I feel His pleasure!" Here was a man that knew his purpose and why. This filled his life with meaning and gave him a residual impact on the world. You can see evidence of the difference Eric made on earth through the award-winning movie and books about his life and from his mission to the people of China before and during World War II. Eric Liddell, a devout Christian missionary, made such an impact wherever he served that even to this day he is revered in communist China.

I have observed that almost everyone wants to know why they are here (purpose) and if they matter (meaning). Knowing, *really knowing*, that God loves and cares for us gives our lives tremendous meaning and comes with the heavenly aroma we call peace and joy. It's a tangible reminder that God is with us, that we have a significant role to play in His great master plan, and when we walk in the plan He has uniquely designed for us, we, like Eric, will feel His pleasure!

Being Part of a Great Master Plan

I love the opening scene in the Disney movie *Beauty and the Beast* where Belle says, "I want adventure in the great wide somewhere… It simply would be grand to have someone understand… I want so much more than they have planned."

We were all born for God to live through us and to further His Kingdom here on earth. This is the adventure I hear Belle crying out for; and I believe that, deep down, all of us have that same yearning.

There is a great master plan playing out all around us, and I would love to see every individual discover their unique personal role in this great universal plan. One reason why I wrote this book is to help others realize that there is so much more to life than we have experienced and where to go if they want more.

To the interested observer there is proof of a master plan

everywhere you look. From the wonder of a starlit sky to the mysteries hidden in our own DNA, a master plan is clearly evident. Whether you think about it or not, you have a deep desire to know why you are here and how and where you fit in the world. Finding your fit in the master plan can go a long way in helping you find purpose, meaning and value in life.

These needs are just as important for us to address for a quality of life as any of our physical or emotional needs. Our current culture has us so focused on the satisfaction of our physical needs that most of our thoughts and efforts are directed toward these pursuits. It is sad to say, but most of us have become so busy trying to provide for the daily requirements of our physical bodies that the pursuit of satisfying these needs through work and pleasure have become the primary source of meaning.

That being said, I believe that if we are ever going to find the real meaning and purpose of our lives we are going to have to, at least for a moment, step off of the daily treadmill of life and shift our focus from our traditional pattern and entertain a question or two out of the norm. The reason why I recommend this is in the hope that each of us can begin to question our current worldview. Once we start to ask ourselves, "What do we really believe and why?", we are starting down a path in which we may discover more about our own personal purpose and unlocking the keys to health, true wealth, and well-being.

Successful People In and Out of the Bible

Every successful person had to face trials and defeats before making it. George Washington had his difficult winter at Valley Forge before he won independence from Britain at Yorktown. Michael Dell was laughed at before he succeeded building The Dell Computer Company. WD-40 took 39 tries before the company got the formula right with the 40th try. I would be able to name countless others who have overcome terrible odds to discover the successful fulfillment of their purpose.

I could also list many Biblical characters who struggled for years before coming into the place God created for them. Joseph spent years in prison before becoming a ruler in Egypt. David also spent years after being anointed King of Israel before he ascended to the throne. There isn't enough time to share with you all the people who had to patiently endure trials before they came into their purpose: Daniel in the lion's den, the Apostle Paul and his trials and persecutions, not to mention all that Jesus went through before He ascended to His throne. Because you have forces opposing the fulfillment of your purpose could be a sign that you are on the right track. Another important point regarding our purpose in life is that even after we've found it, we are still only scratching the surface of all God has for us.

Living out our purpose is more like walking than arriving, and the road may have many twists and turns. We just need to remind ourselves that God is watching every move we make, and if we include Him, He'll help us with the ups and downs. A very wise man, John the Baptist, said regarding the coming of Jesus, that He would see that *"The valleys will be filled, and the mountains and hills made level. The curves will be straightened, and the rough places made smooth." (Luke 3:5)*

I feel it is important that as we journey along our course in life it is critical we keep moving forward, even if we don't fully understand our purpose yet. There's an old saying, "God can't steer a ship that isn't moving." Learning the totality of our "one thing" all at once would be for most of us, overwhelming. Therefore, God usually gives us just enough light to see the next step or two. The main thing at this stage is to keep stepping out in faith, trusting that we will eventually arrive at our destination, the purpose for which we were designed.

How to Discover Your Purpose

Here are some questions to ask yourself to help uncover your purpose in life:

1. What is the most serious problem in the world? One of the solutions or ways to address that problem could point to your purpose.

2. What do you feel really passionate about? What do you love doing and time seems to fly by when you are doing it?

3. What do you care so deeply about that you would risk almost anything to see it fixed or fulfilled? When you see this problem, you wish someone would fix it. You may ask yourself why everyone can't see the seriousness of this issue that you see.

4. In what area are you gifted or talented? When you work or perform in this area you notice it always appears to go well.

5. Is the task you feel called to so big that it can only be done in God's ability?

6. Is there an open door for you to serve somewhere, and would you participate even if you weren't paid?

7. Are you thinking about doing something out of the ordinary? Does this challenge conventional wisdom? Would this work set people free or better their lives? If so, you are likely on the threshold of God's ultimate purpose for your life.

My hope for you is that these questions will help you uncover your purpose so that you will experience more meaning and satisfaction in life.

It's also important to remember that your purpose in life is not a destination or a place where everything is perfect and where there are no problems or struggles.

We all have certain gifts and talents that are part of God's purpose for our lives. However, your "one thing" will likely grow out of God's gift of divine love to you. I wasn't really prepared to meet the man upstairs face-to-face, but His coming downstairs changed everything....

4. THE MAN UPSTAIRS CAME DOWNSTAIRS

One afternoon, "the man upstairs" came downstairs to meet me in my bedroom. I was sitting up in bed completely awake, quietly praying and waiting on God, when all of a sudden Jesus appeared to me hovering over the foot of my bed. He was wearing a long white robe in the middle-eastern style with a brown sash across His chest. He had long brown hair, and I can't say that I saw His face; somehow, I knew, though, beyond a shadow of a doubt that it was the Lord.

He then reached His hand down through my chest, which strangely didn't trouble me at all. When He began to pull His hand back, He was actually holding someone else by the hand and began to pull them up toward Himself through my chest. As I observed this person being pulled up by Jesus, I noticed that he or she was holding on to the hand of another person, who in turn came up through my chest. This next person was also holding on to the hand of another person, and as each individual came up through my chest, they were also holding the hand of another.

This continued for quite some time. As Jesus moved farther and farther away, He eventually faded out of view with a continuous chain of people between us. It reminded me of the old paper dolls that children used to play with.

That experience with the Lord Jesus taught me some very valuable lessons then, and He is still teaching me from this one experience over 25 years later. One lesson is that the most impactful ministry is when we let the Lord do it through us, just like Jesus pulling people to Himself through me. I was just there as a vehicle for Jesus to use and a witness to His ministry. He does all the work and gets all the glory. That's the way all ministry should be.

Another lesson was that all of God's blessings and gifts entrusted to us are more for the benefit of others than for us. If God can get His blessing through us, He'll get it to us!

I am just beginning to see this principle of multiplication that the Lord demonstrated when He appeared to me in my bedroom that day. God has recently revealed that His model of disciple making is not to just make disciples but to teach others how to make disciples, as well. That's the practice that leads to reaching a multitude with the good news of Jesus Christ. God doesn't just want us to be concerned about our children in the faith but also our grandchildren and great grandchildren. A child in the faith is someone that you introduce to the good news that Jesus has taken away their sin and made eternal life available to them. When this person surrenders their life to Jesus, He gives them His life. Actually, all that God has is already ours; people just need us to let them know this good news so that they can receive it.

When someone receives Jesus, they become our child in the faith. As we disciple them, just as a parent guides their child through to maturity, we help these new followers of Jesus to grow in their faith. When our children in the faith share about their relationship with Jesus with others who come to faith in Him, they become our grandchildren in the faith.

The Man Upstairs Concept Can Be a Ditch by the Road

I have experienced the painful reality that most paths in life have ditches on both sides. The concept of God as "the man upstairs" is a ditch on the side of the road. If we look at God as a person like us, we are actually making Him in our image, as I stated before. If God is like us, basically a bigger version of a human being, then He really can't be of much help in a crisis. This is a very common misunderstanding of God (as a larger version of ourselves) and is typical of the kind of thinking that lands us in one of the ditches along the road. There is another mistaken view about God held by millions of people around the world, which is that God can't be human and divine at the same time. This philosophy constitutes a world view that lands people in the ditch on the other side of the road.

If we believe that God is just a larger version of ourselves, we will veer off the road of life into a ditch of self-reliance, self-aggrandizement and self-centeredness; in a nutshell, self for self. If we believe God isn't big enough to help us through anything we may face, then it's all up to us to fix things.

If we believe that God is a distant, uncaring entity or some impersonal force, we'll end up in the ditch on the other side of the road. With this impersonal view of God, we never learn the purpose of our lives because there is no personal Creator to show us. This is the "God doesn't care" ditch. The reality is that if we fall into either ditch we won't end up where we are supposed to be, which is having a life marked by peace, contentment and well-being.

Does God Really Care and Can He Help?

The middle of the road is the only safe place to be. This is walking with God, knowing that He is big enough to help us with any problem we face and that He knows us personally and He cares for us.

The truth is actually very good news. God is both man and God at the same time. Being God He doesn't have the same limitations the rest of mankind has, but since He's also human He can be touched by our frailty and pain.

Humanity came from God in the beginning; but in an act of disobedience and rebellion our progenitors fell from God's favor and had to leave His presence, causing the world to fall into a state of darkness. We have not only inherited their fallen nature with its propensity to sin, but we also live in a fallen and broken world. Due to the fall of humankind we have a spiritual nature that has been separated from God.

Since in our fallen state we can't partake of God's life and love, we turn to earthly pursuits and pleasures of this broken world to try to fill our emptiness. However, nothing in this world can satisfy our loneliness or mend our broken hearts.

In God's master plan Jesus came to pay for our rebellion and evil deeds with His own death on a cross. Jesus then rose from the dead, triumphed over evil, sin and death, and gave us a way back to God through faith in His Son. He also made available the gift of eternal life, God's kind of life, to fill our emptiness and heal our brokenness. God is now with us so that He might be enjoyed in this world and in the next.

In summary, God made a perfect world and placed man in it, giving him dominion. When man disobeyed God he turned that dominion over to the devil. Since God had given the earth to man, He had to become a man to take it back, which He did in the person of Jesus of Nazareth. He paid for our rebellion with His own life and took back dominion in the earth by rising from the dead. Jesus then gave that dominion back to those that would receive Him and believe in His name.

As John the Apostle wrote, *"And this is the testimony: that God has given us eternal life, and this life is in His Son. 12. He who has the Son has life; he who does not have the Son of God does not have life. 13. These things I have written to you who believe in the name of the Son of God, that you may know that you have eternal life, and that you may continue to believe in the name of the Son of God."* (1John Chapter 5:11 – 12)

I contend that our primary purpose as human beings is to receive the life of Jesus within us and to share that life with others. Once we learn that Jesus is real and that having His life can make a difference in our lives here on earth, we ought to let others know that He is real and His life is available to them as well. Once they experience the life of Jesus, they will discover that He is able to help them with anything they'll face in life. This is because He is God and He *wants* to help, for He loves and cares for us. God, "the man upstairs", came downstairs in the person of Jesus so that we can have a relationship with Him.

Yes, there is a "man upstairs"; and His name is Jesus Christ. He is God and one with the Father and the Holy Spirit. Faith in Jesus, God come in the flesh, gives us more meaning and purpose in life than anyone who hasn't experienced it can imagine; and it's available to everyone, everywhere.

Early in my walk with God I discovered that God is an eternal being and that He is the one true God. But I also learned that He exists in three persons - Father, Son and Holy Spirit. You might ask yourself; how can one person be three people?

First of all, the Bible says that *"God is Light."* (1John 1:5) One way to look at it is to observe white light through a prism, which refracts the light into a rainbow of colors. This shows that the white light that we see is one light, but it contains multiple colored lights within. The many lights are united in one, just as the Father contains the Son and the Spirit.

The concept of three persons - Father, Son and Holy Spirit - in one God can be found in multiple places in the Bible, with one of the most obvious being Jesus' baptism. *(Matthew 3:17)* Jesus is being baptized in the River Jordan, the Holy Spirit falls upon Him as a dove, and the Father declares, *"This is my beloved Son in whom I am well pleased."* All three are present as separate persons. The Bible goes on to say, *"For in Him dwells the fullness of the Godhead bodily." (Colossians 2:9)* This means that in Jesus all of God, His entire person and nature, resides. Jesus is God come in the flesh and all of God is in Him. "The man upstairs", Jesus Christ, God in the flesh, came downstairs for you and me.

Concepts like the ones we've been discussing, that God is one in three persons, are beyond human understanding. Only God could come up with something like this, which helps prove that the Bible alone, among all religious books, was inspired by God.

I encountered Jesus' human nature shortly after I was healed by that flash of divine light. I was reading a book about Jesus' crucifixion, the step-by-step suffering He endured before His death and the horrific torture of dying on the cross. As I read the account it all became very real to me. It was as if I was there at the foot of the cross, watching Jesus going through it all. I was moved by His intense sacrifice for me, and I wept uncontrollably as I realized He was doing this for me! In that moment I came to the knowledge of Jesus Christ as my Lord and Savior.

I am reminded of something the Apostle Paul wrote that I believe relates to our encountering Christ's crucifixion and resurrection. *"I have been crucified with Christ; it is no longer I who live, but Christ lives in me; and the life which I now live in the flesh I live by faith in the Son of God, who loved me and gave Himself for me." (Galatians 2:20)*

There's a right way and a wrong way to think about God as "the man upstairs." If we see God as a larger version of ourselves, we'll see Him with limitations. If we see Him as the one true God who took on human flesh to become our deliverer, well that's another story!

When I Asked for the Holy Spirit

A few years later I had another encounter with the real "man upstairs". This one was quite different and so powerful that I haven't shared it with many people. I feel that the Lord wants me to share it now to let you know that visitations like this are possible and to help raise your expectancy.

Jesus comes to every one of His new followers by His Holy Spirit. He will come in us, recreating our spirit into a new spirit in Him. At this time God also places us in Himself as the Apostle John says,*" Whoever confesses that Jesus is the Son of God, God remains in him, and he in God." (1John 4:15)* God will also come upon us in the Holy Spirit. You can see the difference between these two manifestations of the Spirit of God in the lives of Jesus' disciples. After Jesus rose from the dead, all of His disciples were hiding in fear for their lives. Jesus appeared to them and breathed on them, saying, *"Receive the Holy Spirit." (John 20:19-22)* Later on, as Jesus was about to ascend into heaven, He told them that they would receive power after the Holy Spirit came upon them. *(Acts 1:8)* The disciples did receive the Holy Spirit upon them on the day of Pentecost as reported by Luke the physician. *(Acts 2:1 – 17)* I believe that I received the Spirit of Jesus when I confessed that He is Lord and Savior after I was introduced to Him through my first pastor, John Scudder. I have been growing in my understanding of the reality of Christ in me ever since. I received the Holy Spirit "upon" me sometime later after I noticed that the Holy Spirit fell on people in the Bible *(Acts 2:17 "It shall come to pass in the last days, says God, That I will pour out of My Spirit on all flesh; Your sons and your daughters shall prophesy, Your young men shall see visions, Your old men shall dream dreams.; Acts 10:44: "While Peter was still speaking these words, the Holy Spirit fell upon all those who heard the word.")*. One night as I was kneeling in prayer, I asked God that I be filled with the Holy Spirit, and I was!

We lived in an old drafty farm house at the time, and since it was winter in New England the room was quite cold. The Holy Spirit came upon me like a golden cloud of light. His presence was both beautiful and frightening, and it seemed brighter than the sun at noon. I can recall the sweat dripping off my chest because of the intense heat generated by His presence. I didn't know how much longer I could survive in that light so I asked the Lord to lift His presence from me, which He did. I was wishing afterword that I had stayed with Him longer, but it wasn't long before He began returning to me regularly. His presence was like a cloud of light and would come at times as I was in prayer. In my opinion, the presence of God is the most wonderful experience a human being can have on this earth. It is worth more than all the power and riches this world has to offer, and it is available to everyone.

Expecting God to Be God in Our Lives

John Wayne gave some good advice when he said, "When the road looks rough ahead, remember the 'man upstairs' and the word HOPE. Hang onto both and 'tough it out'." However, for this to be really powerful we need to read it in light of what we have learned so far. Yes, when the road ahead in life looks rough it will be very helpful to remember that God is with us and will deliver us. *(Psalm 91:15: "You shall call upon Me, and I will answer You; I will be with you in trouble; I will deliver you and honor you.")* We also need to realize that God is truly *able* to help because His ways and abilities are way beyond ours and that He *wanted* to help by coming downstairs and becoming a man to help us.

John Wayne recommended that we not only hold on to God but also to hope. Why? Isn't hope just wishful thinking? NO! Most people think hope means that we are wishing for something, but what it really means is "confident expectation". When we have hope, what we are saying is that although we don't yet see the answer for what we need or want, the solution is on its way.

Hope means that you are expecting something. It's already yours, although it hasn't yet manifested. When a woman is pregnant, we say she is expecting. If you ask her if she has a child she'll say "yes". But where's the child? The child is in her, and we don't see it yet. That's hope! Expecting what God has promised to manifest in the physical world from the spiritual world is also hope.

The Bible says that we are saved by grace through faith. *(Ephesians 2:8)* The word "saved" means to be delivered from enemies. Many people believe that to be saved means you are only going to heaven, but another wonderful part of salvation is that we can also experience deliverance from our enemies here and now. I think that since being delivered from sin, death and eternal damnation is such a big thing and eternity is such a long time, the enormity of it all blinds us from the other enemies from which we have been saved.

Most of our enemies (fear, worry, hate, sickness, and poverty, among others) are still here, and we need to be saved from them as well. The same way we are delivered from our eternal enemies, like sin, death and the devil, is the way we are delivered from all temporal enemies - by grace through faith. We are saved by grace, the free gift from Jesus, the God-Man who came downstairs to save us from all our enemies. Jesus accomplished this deliverance over 2,000 years ago at His cross and resurrection. This means that all of our enemies have been conquered for us.

As Jesus said, *"Here on earth you will have many trials and sorrows. But take heart, because I have overcome the world." (John 16:33 NLT)* This means that in this world we will face many problems and disappointments; but if we have a relationship with Jesus, He will help us through it all. Jesus said, *"Peace I leave with you, My peace I give to you; not as the world gives do I give to you. Let not your heart be troubled, neither let it be afraid."* (John 14: 28) No matter what we may face, Jesus has made His peace available to us so that we never have to be afraid.

Grace is God's free gift of all that we need and so much more. Faith is our belief that His free gift is already ours, and faith is also the way in which we receive the manifestation of God's gifts here in the physical world.

I hear people say all the time that they or someone they know have faith, but they still haven't been healed of a serious disease or delivered from some other issue that God promised to take care of. These people are right that they have faith because if they have Jesus, who is full of faith, they have all the faith they will ever need.

In my experience, the problem is not that we don't have enough faith but that we have the wrong kind of hope. The Bible says that we are also saved by hope. *(Romans 8:24)* Wishing that God would save us from a problem won't get it done. We have to "expect" that He will do what He promised. This is the true meaning of hope and a huge key to receiving the provision, healing and deliverance that God has made available to us.

God's total, complete and unconditional forgiveness for all of our sin has been bought and paid for by Jesus and is available for everyone. Also, God's eternal life, peace, health and joy are free and waiting for anyone who is willing to receive them. This is what is called the Gospel, the Good News - that Jesus has taken away everything that separated us from God and has given us His life so that we could be reunited with Him NOW - here on earth. All we need to do is to repent and have faith in Jesus. This means believing that His payment for our sin on the cross was enough for our forgiveness and that His resurrection from the dead gave us everlasting life.

Many people misunderstand the definition of repent, as if it means begging God to forgive us or having to do some kind of penance to appease God for our transgressions. Nothing can be farther from the truth. Repent simply means to change your mind. In other words, when we repent and have faith in Jesus, we are simply turning from a mindset of trusting in ourselves to live a good life to trusting Jesus' help and strength to live a good life. In my experience, having Jesus' love, joy and peace here on earth is something so good it really has to be true.

I'm not proud of this, but before I knew Jesus was "for real" and that He loved and accepted me, I used to argue with Christians that God was dead just to mess with them. Many in the world appeared to agree with me....

5. THE REPORTS OF GOD'S DEATH HAVE BEEN EXAGGERATED

"The reports of my death have been greatly exaggerated!" *(Mark Twain)*

I grew up in a household that believed in God. Some of my teachers in high school and in college were professed atheists and a few were even hostile toward God. I remember being required to read books by renowned atheists in some of my college classes. It appeared to me that the atheists made better arguments against God's existence than those who were pro-God made *for* His existence.

The anti-God arguments really fit my way of thinking at the time. I couldn't understand why a loving God would allow such pain and suffering in the world, so I decided that maybe the atheists and those that say God is dead are right.

I later found out that the pro-God people were right and that there were logical reasons why the world was such a mess. However, at the time it appeared to me that most people, at least those at the university, appeared to believe that God was dead.

Is God Dead?

In 1966 the headline on the cover of <u>Time Magazine</u> said, "Is God

Dead?" This article drew from the writings of Friedrich Nietzsche, who in 1882 declared that God was dead. This article was designed to have some shock value so that they could sell more magazines, but it was also indicative of a perceived trend in some religious institutions that scholars were trying to come up with a belief system apart from God.

Some theologians (religious leaders) think it's necessary to come up with a theology (religious system) that is more compatible with a society that, in their view, has been and is becoming more secularized (godless) all the time. It's pretty sad when the religious leaders in a society believe that God is no longer relevant.

Jesus dealt with a similar mindset among the religious leaders of His day. It's so human to want to keep God in a box. If God is in a box, He might as well be dead to us. This is because a God that fits comfortably in a container of our design won't be of much help when the problems and turmoil of life get beyond our control.

There were religious leaders standing right there as Jesus healed a woman who was bent over from severe bone disease. They had put God in a box to a point where they were completely blind to the fact that God was standing right there with them in the person of Jesus. It didn't even register that only God could do the miracle they had just seen. Their religious box only let them see that Jesus had broken the rules, and they were ready to kill Him for it! Here's Luke's account of what happened:

The meeting-place president, furious because Jesus had healed on the Sabbath, said to the congregation, "Six days have been defined as work days. Come on one of the six if you want to be healed, but not on the seventh, the Sabbath."

15-16 But Jesus shot back, "You frauds! Each Sabbath every one of you regularly unties your cow or donkey from its stall, leads it out for water, and thinks nothing of it. So why isn't it all right for me to untie this daughter of Abraham and lead her from the stall where Satan has had her tied these eighteen years?" (Luke 13:14 – 16 MSG)

My primary concern regarding people believing that God is dead is not for those who doubt or deny His existence. My main concern is for those of us who actually believe that God is alive but live as if He isn't. At least atheists are authentic in their stand that there is not a God or that He is dead. When a person is honest about their atheistic beliefs and have an encounter with the power of God as I did, they'll often be as sold out *for* God as they were *against* Him.

The Life We Live Is a Direct Result of Our Beliefs

If everyone who says they are a believer in God lived as if they really believed that He was with them all the time, the world would be a much better place. That's how the early Christians reached their whole known world in a few generations. The early believers in Jesus were so sold out for God and so aware of His presence with them that they turned the world upside-down. When the plague came through town they stayed and ministered to the sick with no thought for themselves, because God was with them. When natural disasters or war broke out, they helped the hurting, those orphaned, in prison or widowed. They showed the unconditional love and power of God and drew their world to Christ.

We could do the same thing today if we believe the incredible truths in the Bible about how God wants to live His life through us to further His Kingdom in this world. Sadly, with many Christians this is not the case. For many, God is as good as dead, stored in a box or kept as a distant historical reference. In our society today God isn't called upon much to make a difference, even in the lives of believers.

Take marriage for example. The divorce rate for believers is almost exactly the same as it is for non-believers. I'm not saying that abusive relationships never happen or that someone in a terrible or adulterous relationship has to stay in that relationship. However, if the partners in more marriages really believed that there is a personal, living God who loves them and is there to help them love and care for one another, I believe that the divorce rate would drop.

If we really believe that God is alive and that He is aware of everything we are thinking or doing, wouldn't this world be very different? I believe it would! If we knew God was standing right next to us we probably would be less likely to gossip, lie or steal. However, God didn't come to this earth, die on a cross and rise from the dead so that we would be better behaved!

In fact, He said, *"I have kept my Fathers commandments." (John 15:10)* Jesus kept God's commandments for us because not one of us could ever keep them all anyway. He kept them for us and died to pay the penalty for our breaking them. Jesus did say that we should keep *His* commandments. His commands are love God and love each other *(1 John 4: 21)*. That's it! In keeping these commands, we won't break the others. If you love someone you won't gossip about them, lie to them, steal from them or do anything contrary to that love.

Ironically, it's actually impossible to love everyone without the love and the power of God in us. This is important because it keeps us focused on God. We can't live the life we are called to live without Him being alive and active in us.

Why Did Jesus Come?

Jesus did not come to make us better behaved. One of the main reasons He came was to give us His life and life even more abundantly. *(John 10:10)* God knows that if we come to Him for His life and stay plugged into Him on a continual basis, His life flowing through us will help us be better people.

Where do we find this life? It's found in a living, vital relationship with God through His Son Jesus. As Jesus said, *"Now this is eternal life: that they know you, the only true God, and Jesus Christ, whom you have sent." (John 17:3)* Jesus is saying here that eternal life, God's kind of life, is found in knowing Him and the Father. The word "know" in this Scripture comes from a Greek word meaning "intimacy". The life of God comes to us through an intimate relationship with God and His Son Jesus.

Jesus also said, *"If you abide in me, and my words abide in you, ask whatever you wish, and it will be done for you." (John 15:7)* Jesus was simply saying that life is what we need, and it is found in His presence. He also wanted us to know that if we dwell in Him and His words dwell in us, we will want what He wants. We will naturally ask for things in line with His will; therefore, God will give us all that we ask for.

Jesus, in referring to His words, said, *"The words that I speak to you are spirit, and they are life". (John 6:63)* Is it that simple? Do I just have to turn to the words in the Bible to find life? If this is the case, how do I trust what it says? If the Bible is the written word of God and the true source of life, how do I access it? These were the questions I was wrestling with shortly after the miraculous healing I experienced.

I was told by my first pastor that the Bible was inspired by God and was the only book that could be fully trusted. He said that I could count on it to always guide me in the right direction. I was wondering, how could I prove this for myself? How could I know that the Bible was the inspired word of God to me? I had the thought that since there are many prophesies in the Old Testament about the coming of the Jewish Messiah, and if they were fulfilled by Jesus in the New Testament, then Jesus was who He said He was, the Son of God. This would also prove that the Bible was inspired by God because how else could the authors know that all these events would happen centuries later?

I couldn't be sure that the early Christians did not doctor the Old Testament to fit Jesus' life, but I knew that the Jews would not have made any changes. My next step brought me to some Jewish book stores to check out their Bible. I wasn't fully prepared for what I found. The Jewish Bible had the same books as the Christian Bible, and after careful review I found that there were over 60 major prophesies about the Messiah and over 200 minor ones that were fulfilled by Jesus.

This blew me away! For example, Israel's King David wrote in Psalm 22 about the Messiah that soldiers would divide his garments among themselves, gamble for his cloak and that His bones would be out of joint, which all happened when Jesus was hung on the cross. How did David know that these things would happen to Jesus over 1,000 years before His death?

The Jewish prophet Micah prophesied 700 years before Jesus was born that His birthplace would be in the village of Bethlehem. How could Jesus have made that happen? Another was the prophet Isaiah who wrote in chapter 53 of his book 700 years before Jesus was born that He would be whipped and that He would be wounded for our transgressions. These are just a few examples of the many prophesies in the Jewish Bible that were fulfilled in one man, Jesus Christ.

I read that a statistician once calculated the probability of some of these prophesies being fulfilled in one person. He calculated that the chances that Jesus might <u>not</u> be the Messiah, with just eight of the more than 260 prophesies fulfilled by Him, to be 1 in 100 quadrillion. (More Than a Carpenter by Josh McDowell)

There are many other proofs that confirm that Jesus is God come in the flesh, but the fulfillment of these prophesies settled the question for me once and for all about Jesus' divinity and the Bible's authenticity.

I had personal proof of the divinity of Jesus and the truth of the Bible. I had already been healed of a serious malady and also had come to know Jesus on a personal basis. He was now as real to me as any friend or family member. I could never deny that He had become my closest and most trusted companion.

How I Began My Quest to Know God Better

I was reading Psalm 46 in the Bible one day and noticed that it said, *"Be still and know that I am God"*. I realized that if I could be still, I might get to know God better. At the beginning I had a really difficult time sitting still, so I began to set an egg timer for five minutes to train my body and mind to be still. I tried not to move, scratch or swallow and kept my mind focused on God. It was the longest five minutes ever! After a couple weeks of diligent practice, I mastered the five minutes and moved on to 10 minutes, then 15.

When I got to 20 minutes of being still, I would begin to see a bright cloud off in the distance while my eyes were closed. I knew that it was the Holy Spirit. As He drew closer, I could actually feel His presence on my skin and entering into my body. What glory it is to be touched by the living God! It is a foretaste of heaven on earth, and I can't imagine living a day without His tangible touch. These encounters with God's Spirit only intensified my desire to better understand the Bible, seek God's presence and please Him in all I do.

From the moment I first encountered God's presence, the way in which I viewed the world began to change. It was as if everything turned upside-down. This transition reminded me of the scene in the movie *The Matrix* where Morpheus offers Neo a choice. "Take the blue pill and stay the way you are and believe whatever you want to or take the red pill and I'll show you how deep the rabbit hole goes" (obviously a reference to Alice in Wonderland's new reality). Morpheus then says, "Remember I'm only offering you the truth."

Truth is another word for "reality". Morpheus was offering to take Neo to the real world. Remember that Jesus told Pilot, "I have come into the world, that I should bear witness to the truth." Jesus was telling Pilot, the Roman governor, that this world was only a shadow of the real and that Jesus came from the real (true) world *(John 18: 37)*.

When Neo awoke in the real world, he found that everyone, including himself, was plugged into a virtual reality that made them all slaves. After I woke up to the truth that God is real, just like Neo waking up from the false reality that had imprisoned him, there was no going back to my old life.

At this point, if I was going to live my life the way I used to, I would have to act as if God were dead, even though I knew He was very much alive. We humans do this all the time because it can be uncomfortable to be sold out for God. For example, sometimes I get angry! It is sad to say, but since it feels good, I ignore God's voice (as if He were dead) and indulge my anger. I eventually give in to His voice and turn from my poor self-control, but it's still not the best way to behave or the way I want to behave.

Another example is when God called me to go on a mission trip to Africa. I didn't want to go, so I dug in my heels and delayed going for over a year. Eventually I went to Rwanda, Africa. I only wish I had done it sooner because it was a life-changing experience for me and set the foundation for my current ministry. I should have gone when God first told me to go. It would have been better for me because I would have avoided the stress that pushing against God's will usually causes.

We often act as if God's not there. We know that He's not dead but act as if He is. We ignore whole passages from the Bible that are not compatible with our understanding. We resist God's inner leading if it's not in line with what we want to do in the moment. I don't know about you, but I'm pretty stubborn when it comes to being told to do something that I don't understand or want to do. Thankfully, I am learning to be more sensitive to His leading and to respond more quickly. Everything tends to go better when I do.

I've heard it said that the safest place in the world is to be in the middle of God's plan. I believe that to be true. Some believe God won't protect us if we're not in His perfect spot. I believe that He takes care of me wherever I am. Being in God's perfect plan at the right time allows me to exercise more faith in my life, which He knows is better for me!

In *The Matrix*, as Neo grew in the knowledge of who he really was, his faith was released more and more. He saved his mentor (Morpheus) and his girlfriend (Trinity), and as his friends watched his incredible exploits, they made comments like, "He's beginning to believe" or "He is the One".

As Neo grew in the knowledge of who he was, his ability to do miracles grew, too. It's the same way with us. As the things Jesus said about us become more real to us, we begin to release more faith, and we begin to believe and act more like Him. Jesus said, *"Most assuredly, I say to you, he who believes in Me, the works that I do he will do also; and greater works than these he will do, because I go to My Father." (John 14:12)*

Jesus said that if we believe in Him, we will do what He did. This would be true of every believer in Jesus, wouldn't it? How can we read this and act as if He's dead? We need to grab a hold of what Jesus said and live as if He really meant it. If we do this one thing, we will change our world.

I already mentioned a few times that God intervened in my life with miraculous healings. This is my story, and it's as real to me as anything in this world. I can't tell you how many times someone has told me that God doesn't heal any more. Many have bought into the lie propagated by certain religious leaders who say that miracles passed away with Jesus and His immediate disciples. If they were correct in believing that miracles passed away, I would have already passed away. I'm living proof that nothing could be further from the truth. These leaders live their lives and teach others as if miracles were for yesterday. In this area of God's blessing, therefore, He is as good as dead to them.

Fortunately, God is very much alive! Not only does He heal the sick today as He did 2,000 years ago, but He does it through us. God has placed the Spirit of His Son Jesus in the heart of every believer, and we are able to do the works that Jesus did in this present world. Little by little, we can and should help other people wake up to the good news about Jesus and how His power and love can transform this world one person at a time.

I didn't know how soon this truth would be needed in my family.

6. MY WIFE AND SONS NEED MIRACLES

I was attending a meeting near my home when a man approached me with some very serious health concerns. He said that someone suggested we talk. I asked him, "What is the problem?" He replied that he had been treated for prostate cancer. They placed radioactive seeds into his prostate. The radiation burned through his prostate and rectum. He was told that since the wound was cauterized (scarred by burning) that it would never heal, that he would need to be on morphine and he would be bleeding for the rest of his life.

I told him, "I pray for people and God heals them. Would you like me to pray for you?" He said he would. We located an empty room near where the group was meeting. I placed my hands on him and told the pain and bleeding to stop. I asked that the healing Jesus provided to manifest in his body. We then waited for God's presence to touch him. He said that he felt a heat while I prayed. He thanked me and went home. A few days later he stopped by to see me. He was so excited! The pain and bleeding were gone and the wound was completely healed. It was a miracle!

God Broadens My "One Thing"

After I was healed by a touch from God, I learned that healing was part of what God wanted for us. I also found that God's presence, power and authority can really make a difference here on earth, including in the area of health and healing. He wanted me to learn how to use His healing power to show people that God loves them and to help them become more open to the Gospel of the Kingdom. I found that when I prayed for people who felt a healing touch from God that they wanted to find out more about Jesus and the difference He could make in their lives. This helped expand my understanding of my "one thing". Not only was I a person with Christ living through me, but He was using me to fulfill His purpose of furthering His Kingdom in this world.

Not long after my own encounter with the power of God and the resulting healing I experienced, my wife, who was expecting our second child, became quite ill and needed a healing miracle, too. It's pretty hard to tell a story about God's intervention in my life without referencing His miraculous healing power.

Our World was Turned Upside-down

I wasn't the only one whose life was totally changed that night in my 25th year when I was healed by being thrown into the Light. This also had quite an impact on my family, especially my wife Kathy. The first indication that something had changed in me was that I was reading books instead of watching T.V. I read books about God, health, finance, spirituality and many other topics. I began to see the world in a very different way. Since I had been healed by an unimaginably powerful presence that was obviously beyond this natural world, I knew there was something of which I had not been aware of before. This new understanding was turning my wife's and my world upside-down. There was a reality beyond my five senses that possessed immense power, and I wanted to learn more about it.

I began to see that there were two realities going on here at the same time - the physical world I knew all my life and the spiritual world, to which I was just awakening. Because of the dawning within me of the reality of God, His presence began to become much more tangible to me. I could actually sense Him around me and even feel His love. I felt very blessed and favored. It was like I had just been unplugged from an alternative dimension, like Neo waking up from the Matrix; and just like Neo, I could never go back to being who I used to be.

My Wife Needed a Miracle

This transformation was happening so quickly that it was putting a lot of stress on my pregnant wife. Toward the end of her pregnancy she began to retain water, and it was affecting her blood pressure. The doctor ordered her to be admitted to the hospital where she could rest. He told me that he was worried about her and the baby. Though it was three weeks early, he said that if she didn't go into labor on her own the next day, they would take the baby by C-section. I knew that was not what we wanted. I needed to go home, pray and seek God for answers. I was pretty new in my spiritual journey, and I didn't know what to do or how healing worked. I opened my new Bible and started reading Psalms. After quite some time reading, I came to Psalm 107 and read, *"He sent forth His word and healed them and delivered them from all their destructions"* and *"Oh that men would praise the Lord for His goodness and for His wonderful works unto the children of men."* As I read these verses, it was like they came to life on the page and in my heart. These truths suddenly became more real than all the problems we were facing, and I knew that I knew that everything was going to be all right.

This was my first experience of God's words from the Bible coming alive in my heart, but since then I have found this to be the key of keys for deliverance from every problem we may face in this world. Jesus said, *"The words that I speak to you are spirit, and they are life." (John 6:63)* When we read and ponder God's Word to the point where it literally comes alive with His life it transforms us from the inside out, and whatever problem we are facing begins to fade.

When these truths from Psalm 107 came alive in my heart that dark, desperate night when my wife and unborn child were in the hospital, it was as if God was right there in the room with me. There was nothing separating us, and I knew in that moment that He would give me whatever I asked. I knelt and asked Him that my child would be born that day. I thanked Him, picked myself up and went to bed, glancing at the clock. It was midnight.

I received a phone call from my wife at 7:30 am the next morning letting me know that I had a son. She said that he was perfectly normal – just under 6 lbs. and 18-1/2 in. long. I asked, "When did you go into labor?" She replied, "At 12:05 this morning, but I slept through it all until 6:30 a.m." God answered my prayer five minutes after I asked Him and delivered to us another miracle - a beautiful baby boy we named James.

Unfortunately, our euphoria was short lived. Kathy continued to gain water, even after Jim's birth. This began to really worry the doctors. During the next few days she gained about 50 lbs. of water outside of her cells. She was actually drowning in water while the cells in her body were dying of thirst. Kathy then began to go into organ system failure from the advancing toxemia that was affecting her body. The doctor came to me and said that there was nothing he could do and wanted to send her to the state university medical center. My answer was no way! He already told me there was nothing more he could do. He was quite upset with me and wrote in his log that I had refused medical care and advice. I decided at that point to totally trust God with this situation.

I asked the doctor to leave us alone for a while. A friend and I prayed for Kathy while also laying hands on her. All I said was, "God please heal my wife in Jesus' name. Amen." As I was praying, I could see her catheter bag only had a tiny bit of sticky, bloody discharge in it. When I said, "Amen", the bag completely filled with water!

The doctor returned in a of couple hours and could not believe the change. He said, "The body is an amazing thing". A few days later, just before my wife and son were to be released from the hospital, the doctor stopped by and asked her, "Do you think God healed you?" She replied, "Yes, I know He did!" Only eight days after our son was born, Kathy lost all 50 lbs. of excess water and was back to her pre-pregnancy weight!

Isn't God gracious? I had only been on this journey with Him for a little over a year and had already experienced, personally and with two members of my immediate family, being saved by His amazing grace and power. I knew then that not only did God love me, but I can trust Him no matter what comes my way.

Now I wanted to get to know God more and more intimately and learn all that I could about how His authority and power operate in this world. Since He intervened in my life by saving my family and me, I really owed Him everything. I also had a growing sense of His abiding presence, especially when I prayed. After this experience, I began to seek God about how He might want to use me to help further His Kingdom here on earth.

God Heals My Older Son

God isn't limited to healing one way. The way God healed our son was very different than the way He had healed me, but over the years it has been the way I have seen God's healing manifest most frequently.

When our older son Jeff was about six years old, he was playing on an old farm wagon we had. He stepped on a board that had a rusty nail in it, which went through his foot. A short time later he began to develop white pustules on the roof of his mouth and was showing symptoms of (tetanus) lockjaw. I knew that this was very serious, even life threatening.

One evening around 10 pm after Jeff had fallen asleep, I went in, knelt by his bedside, and gently placed my hands on him. I spoke to the sickness and told it to leave. This I learned from how Jesus healed Peter's mother-in-law in Luke 4:39, where He commanded the fever to leave her body and it did.

Then I commanded tetanus, lockjaw, all infection and disease to leave Jeff's body. I then asked God to heal him in Jesus name. I knew that I had authority over sickness in my son through Jesus and that if I asked God to heal him, He would send healing as soon as I asked.

Then I needed to wait until my son's healing would manifest physically. I have learned that God answers our prayers as soon as we ask them as long as they are in line with His will. I also learned that since Jesus healed everyone who came to Him, He will heal anyone we ask Him to. I just knelt by Jeff's bedside waiting for the manifestation of the healing, thanking God over and over again for what He had already done.

The Answer Came in the Morning

About 2 am a cloud of golden light came down upon my son and me as I was kneeling by his bedside. The presence of God hovered there for a minute or so and vanished. I knew that Jeff was healed so I went to bed rejoicing. In the morning the pustules and the pain were all gone. The healing had fully manifested.

I discovered that prayer and healing are complicated. God always wants to bless and heal His children. However, we have an enemy in the world who wants to prevent our receiving from God. This is just like Daniel when He prayed for an answer from God and a demonic power prevented it from manifesting for 21 days (Daniel 10: 12 – 13).

I also have learned that we have all the faith we need to receive from God if we have Jesus. After all, Jesus said that if we have the smallest amount of faith, like a mustard seed, we could even move mountains *(Mark 11: 23)*.

My problem in not seeing my son healed more quickly wasn't because I didn't have enough faith. I believe it was due to the devil trying to keep my prayer from being answered or my own doubt and unbelief.

I noticed this truth in the story of Peter walking on water. When Peter saw Jesus walking on the water he asked if he could join Him. Jesus said "Come". Peter immediately jumped out of the boat and began walking out to Jesus on the water.

Peter was doing fine until he took his attention off of Jesus and His word and placed it on the stormy winds and waves. Peter then began to sink. Peter's faith in Jesus was all he needed to walk on water as long as he kept his focus on Him. When Peter's focus became divided, he began to sink because the unbelief created in Peter's heart by focusing on the storm caused his faith to short-circuit. (Matthew 14: 28 – 31)

One of the most important things I learned about receiving from God is that we live in two realities at the same time. One I call the physical world; the other reality I call the spiritual world. Our five senses tell our hearts that the physical world is real. The Bible and the Holy Spirit are given to us to reveal the truth to our hearts that the spiritual world is a higher reality than the physical world. God is a Spirit, so the spiritual realm is the source of the physical world and, therefore, the dominant reality. However, the devil and our senses are always lying to us that the physical world is all there is.

We live in a kind of tension between these two worlds, both vying for dominance in our hearts. The reality we focus on the most will become the one we prefer and our dominant reality.

I try to keep this in mind, as I spend most of my time with the world trying to convince me that it is the only reality. Some day you may make a discovery, as I did, that there is another world more real and powerful than anything in this world, which will change your whole perspective on life.

When my wife and I were told by the doctor that if she didn't go into labor right away and that they would take the baby, even though it was still three weeks early, I knew we were in a crisis. I was aware that everything around me was screaming that Kathy and the baby were in big trouble. These were the "facts". I went home from the hospital that night (our son Jeff was only two years old at the time and I needed to be home with him) and turned from the "facts" at the hospital to God, looking for help. I began to read the Psalms from the Bible out loud. As I mentioned before, when I got to Psalm 107 the words literally came alive in my heart. In that moment the reality of God's Kingdom, His promise of healing and deliverance, became more real to my heart than the false reality of the facts of this world. I asked God to save my wife and child, and He did.

When Jeff stepped on the rusty nail and developed the symptoms of lockjaw (tetanus), the pain he felt and the pustules in his mouth were the facts. They were a reality in this world. However, there is a higher reality in the spirit that supersedes the reality or facts of this world. The danger my son was in and the physical pain and symptoms he was experiencing were crying out in my heart and mind that they were the reality.

I knew that when I prayed for Jeff to be healed God sent the healing he needed. I had to wait until, like Peter, my focus was fully on God and His promise and not on the problem.

The truth that Jesus' healing had already been provided for Jeff in this situation was also a reality. The Bible says that *"by His wounds we WERE healed."* (1Peter 2:24) What we see, touch and feel is true here; but there is a greater reality that exists at the same time in the spiritual world called the Truth. The Spirit of Truth is here to bring into manifestation the healing that is already ours because of Jesus' wounds.

When the reality of God's healing for my son's illness that was already available in the Spirit became more real to my heart than the physical symptoms, his healing began to manifest in his physical body by the presence of the Holy Spirit.

It slowly dawned on me that God has already provided all that we need. When God's Word from the Bible comes alive in our hearts by the Holy Spirit, it releases God's life and the conditions will begin to improve. This is because we are displacing the false reality of our senses with the Truth, which releases faith in what God has promised. As I have applied this principle in my life it has brought deliverance many times, in myriad ways, for me and for those whom I've counseled.

Another Healing Needed

For the most part I have lived in good health, but from time to time I have needed healing because some sickness or injury surfaced in my body. Most of the time I just speak to the symptom, tell it to get out in the name of Jesus, and it leaves. Once in a great while when a malady lingers, I get away and meditate on God's Word and His presence until the symptoms leave. Sometimes the "evil one" fights harder than at other times; but I just persist, knowing that I have the victory over sickness through Jesus.

A very serious health issue happened to me once when I was bitten by a spider under my right arm sometime during the afternoon. The following day I developed a temperature of 103 degrees, had red v-shaped blotches spreading across my chest, my whole body was beginning to get a red, blotchy, swollen rash, and my equilibrium was off. I knew that I was in a life-threatening situation, so I went to the Urgent Care Facility near my home. They kept me waiting in an examination room for what seemed like an eternity. While waiting for the doctor I began to pray, focusing on Jesus and His promises and my fever broke. By the time the doctor came in I was feeling much better, so I thanked him and left.

After arriving home, I found a quiet place and waited for God's presence. I did what King David wrote about in Psalm 25 when he said, *"To You, O Lord, I lift up my soul."* Shortly after that the other symptoms began to mend and by morning I was completely healed.

On the rare occasions when I am wrestling with some illness trying to attach itself to me, I get away to a quiet room and begin reading verses in the Bible about God's promises for healing and deliverance. I also ask myself these questions:

> What do these promises mean to me?
>
> Are they true? Yes!
>
> Are they real and for me? Yes!
>
> Is the Bible true? Yes!

When did sickness come into the world? It began at the disobedience of Adam.

Did God in the person of Jesus pay for Adam's disobedience and conquer death and disease already? Yes!

Has God forgiven all iniquities, including mine, and healed all disease, including mine? *(Psalm 103)* Yes!

Whenever I'm wrestling with an illness, I begin by settling these questions in my mind. I start to think about the verses in the scriptures that say that Jesus already healed us, that His words are Spirit and life, that His Spirit is here to quicken our bodies and that the Word is medicine to all our flesh. (1Peter 2:24; Psalm 103: 3; John 6:63; Proverbs 4:22) I continue to meditate and speak God's Word over and over until, eventually, what God said in His Word becomes more real to me than any physical symptoms I might have been experiencing. Before too long I am completely symptom free!

Some people might say that healing was just for when Jesus and the Apostles were alive to show who they were. Some believe that there was a special time for healing and miracles called the Dispensation and that it is long past. They are led to these conclusions because they've never seen a miracle. However, nothing could be further from the truth; my family and I are living proof! I believe that what Jesus said, "The works I do you will do also", is just as true for His followers. *(John 14:12)*

One really important thing I learned was that we need to trust what God says in the Bible more than what people say. If Jesus says that those that believe in Him will do what He did, we should expect as believers to do what He did, even if it hasn't happened for us yet.

Others might say that God gives us sickness. How does someone who is full of life give sickness? Sickness and disease are at times the result of people acting outside of God's will for them. This places them out of God's life, and they can receive judgement in the form of illness and pain. The wonderful thing is that Jesus took on our judgement and the sicknesses that can result from it. *"<u>Christ has redeemed us from the curse of the law</u>, having become a curse for us for it is written, "Cursed is everyone who hangs on a tree""* (Galatians 3:13).

If you knew someone who gave people sicknesses like cancer or some other serious disease, what would you think of that person? What if they had the power to stop someone from getting sick, but they allowed them to get sick anyway? Would you be drawn to them? Would you want to be like them? We shouldn't blame God for doing these things. If God wanted some people sick, why did Jesus (who IS God) heal everyone who came to Him? Jesus never told anyone to stay sick. He was moved with compassion concerning people's sufferings and alleviated them wherever He went.

I used to think that sickness, disease, and other calamities came from God. This misconception turned me into a professed atheist until I read in the Bible, *"Don't be deceived, my dear brothers and sisters. Every good and perfect gift is from above, coming down from the Father of the heavenly lights, who does not change like shifting." (James 1:16 – 17)* I found out that good things like health, true wealth and well-being come from God. Bad things like sickness and poverty come from somewhere else. We need to stop blaming God for the bad things that happen. He has the answer to every problem we face, so it's important to realize that He is the solution to the problem, not the source of the problem.

Still others wonder if it is God's will to heal. I can assure you that it is <u>always</u> God's will to heal. In fact, He already did! Yes, it is God's will that you be healed because He already placed your sickness on Jesus at His death and resurrection. If Jesus provided our healing 2,000 years ago, then it was and is God's will that all sickness be healed. *(Isaiah 53, Matthew 8:17, 1 Peter 2:24, Psalm 103, Ephesians 1:3)*

I am sometimes asked, "Why then isn't everyone healed?" Healing is available to everyone. We might not know that Jesus has included healing through His death and resurrection. We may not feel worthy to receive God's healing because we are so programmed to perform for what we want from others, including God. Maybe it's as simple as the fact that the problem or the pain is so real that it clouds our ability to trust God for a supernatural solution.

I have found that it is usually only after the suffering has gone beyond the capabilities of human intervention to fix that we finally turn to God as our last hope. It's at this point that most of the miracles I've seen have happened. This is because we are now focused on the ultimate answer, God. When we learn to turn to Him sooner, before we hit rock bottom, things tend to go much better for us in crisis situations.

A Few Key Things I learned about Healing

Here are seven things I have learned that have helped me walk in more divine health and healing:

1. Sickness came in at the fall and was healed at the whipping post of Jesus.

Galatians 3:13 Christ has redeemed us from the curse of the law, having become a curse for us, for it is written, "Cursed is everyone who hangs on a tree".

1Peter 2: 24b "By whose (Jesus) stripes you were healed"

2. We are already healed! We need to <u>receive</u> the manifestation of the healing Jesus already provided in our minds and physical bodies.

1 Peter 2:24 who Himself bore our sins in His own body on the tree, that we, having died to sins, might live for righteousness—by whose stripes you were healed.

3. We can command sickness to leave.

Luke 4:38 – 39 ³⁸ Now He (Jesus) arose from the synagogue and entered Simon's house. But Simon's wife's mother was sick with a high fever, and they made request of Him concerning her. ³⁹ So He stood over her and rebuked the fever, and it left her. And immediately she arose and served them.

4. Healing is a free gift available for everyone, paid for by Jesus.

Mark 16:17 – 18 ¹⁷ And these signs will follow those who believe: In My name they will cast out demons; they will lay hands on the sick, and they will recover."

5. We walk in divine health by receiving more of God's life in the physical realm.

Romans 8:11 But if the Spirit of Him who raised Jesus from the dead dwells in you, He who raised Christ from the dead will also give life to your mortal bodies through His Spirit who dwells in you.

6. Jesus is the healer, not us!

A. *Acts 3:16 And His name (Jesus), through faith in His name, has made this man strong, whom you see and know. Yes, the faith which comes through Him (Jesus) has given him (this man) this perfect soundness in the presence of you all.*

7. Faith to receive health and healing is simply to recognize it is already ours, and healing begins to manifest when the reality of the Word comes alive in our hearts.

Philemon 1:6 ...the communication of your faith may become effectual by the acknowledging of every good thing which is in you in Christ Jesus.

John 6:63b ...the words that I speak to you are spirit, and they are life.

I found that a lot of what I learned about healing runs contrary to the microwave society we live in, where sound bites and tweets are where we get a lot of our information and from which we form our opinions. However, I discovered that health, healing and walking with God doesn't work that way. We can't do a quick prayer and expect an instant remedy to everything holding us back from the life we've always wanted. A meaningful and fulfilling life is not a destination but a journey with God, and that takes time and focus.

I Found My "One Thing" and a Key to the Kingdom

Walking with God is an adventure and a big part of what I found to be a key to the Kingdom and my "one thing". As my intimate relationship with God grew, I eventually came to know my "one thing", which is the reality of God living His life through me in this world. This led to a more thorough understanding of Kingdom authority here on earth and of *"Christ in me the hope of glory" (Colossians 1: 27)* Now that I had found my "one thing", it didn't mean that everything would instantly be perfect. It did mean, however, that my life became more purposeful and rewarding.

Jesus said, "Seek first the Kingdom of God and His righteousness and all these things will be given to you." *(John 6: 33)* Knowing that God rewards those that diligently seek Him *(Hebrews 11:6)* and that He is with us and will never leave us *(Hebrews 13.5)* is more valuable than all the money in the world.

It wasn't long before knowing that God was always with me and would take care of me would be put to the test.

7. MY JOURNEY TO HEAVEN AND HELL

"Before the throne there was as it were a sea of glass, like crystal." (St. John)

One night I visited Hell and the next night, Heaven.

While I was meditating on God's presence, I found myself in the spirit just outside a realm of darkness. I believe that it was one of the levels of Hell. The darkness was so thick it felt like you could cut it with a knife. The place was so crowded that I couldn't see any separation between the multitude of the beings that were there. There was no light, love or goodness in that place. It felt as if this realm of darkness was infinite in all directions and there was no light, peace or beauty there. Nowhere else on earth that I have ever been is as awful as that wretched place. I desired to leave, so the Lord brought me back to my living room.

People have asked me, "Were you in your body or in the spirit?" I tell them that I believe I was in the spirit, but it felt like I was in my body. I believe that I was taken to Hell but that it wasn't the deepest part of Hell. I don't know how I know this, but it's worse than any place on earth; and I saw enough to know that I didn't want to go back there or see anyone else go there.

King David writes about the lowest Hell. *(Psalm 86:13)* This would seem to indicate that there is more than one level of Hell. Jesus told a story of a rich man in a place of fire He called Hell, or Hades in Greek. *(Luke 16:23-24)* I knew that the place I visited was Hell but it wasn't burning. I assume that there are even worse parts deeper into Hell than where I was taken, and I'm grateful this was all I saw.

Visiting the Crystal Sea

The next evening, I was again meditating on the Lord when suddenly, at the base of my spine, a ball of yellow energy exploded, releasing a very bright liquid light that instantly surged up my spine, literally exploding in my brain. As this happened, I found myself out of my body, expanding in all directions and hurling through space at a velocity that seemed faster than the speed of light. I remember looking back at the earth, and it was as small as a marble hanging in space. As I continued to fly toward Heaven, even the whole physical universe itself became very small.

The next thing I knew I was standing on a seemingly infinite ocean. The water was like liquid crystal that was both alive and on fire. I could feel life and love emanating from the water. The love coming from the water felt higher and more holy than any love I felt on earth. I found it cleansing and uplifting as this love permeated my being. I had only felt this intense kind of life and love once before in the presence of Jesus. When I saw the Crystal Sea *(Revelation 15:2)* my first thought was about the blood of Jesus that cleansed the heavens. I wished I could have stayed there forever, but as I became aware of my body sitting in my living room back on earth, I was drawn back to it.

What a feeling of smallness as I became fully aware of my body! I often think about that experience, trying to remember how big I felt when I was in the spirit on the Crystal Sea. It reminds me that the cares and struggles of this life are insignificant when compared to what is waiting for us in the heavenly realms.

I have known people and read several accounts of others who have had this experience. One was my first pastor, who began to exhibit a very tangible anointing after his trip to the Crystal Sea. After receiving this new anointing, he saw many more people healed through his ministry. The way this tangible healing power flowed through my pastor reminded me of the Apostle Peter when sick people were laid near him so that they would be healed as he walked by, due to the divine presence of God flowing through him.

Everyone Meditates

I had these experiences while meditating on God and His presence. I usually like to start my mediations by focusing on thanking Jesus for all He has done for me. Meditation is an important key to spiritual growth from the Bible. King David wrote that he meditated day and night on God's word *(Psalm 1: 2)*, and God told Joshua to meditate on His word so that he would be prosperous and have good success *(Joshua 1: 8)*.

By the way, everyone meditates. Most of the time it's called worry! If we spent less time worrying about things we can't control and meditating on God and His promises instead, our lives would change. Worry is really meditating on our problems. If we just change the focus of our thoughts from our problems to our blessings and meditate on those over and over in our minds, everything in our lives would improve.

After my experience at the Crystal Sea I found myself spending less time in meditation, and I was less interested in seeking spiritual revelations. I still studied the Bible, prayed and served in the ministry; but I didn't have the unquenchable thirst for more of God that I had had prior to my visit to the Crystal Sea. It was like achieving a goal and not knowing what to do next.

The "next" came when God in His graciousness opened a wonderful revelation from His Word for me that I call the grace awakening, after the title of the book by Chuck Swindoll. The Bible calls this "being established in grace". *(Hebrews 13:9)*

Established in Grace

The revelation of being established in grace is one of the most important experiences I have ever had in my life. It changed everything for me! For the first time I felt unconditionally loved and forgiven by God. I knew without a doubt that because of what Jesus did for me I was free from guilt and sin, burdens that I had been carrying for most of my Christian walk.

Being established in grace isn't something I learned or earned. It was a revelation and a gift from God and the most precious thing I have. It's not my "one thing" or the Kingdom of God, but it makes them possible in my life. You might say that being established in grace opens the door to God's Kingdom here on earth. This is because knowing that the Creator of the universe loves us and that nothing can come between us means that "If God be for me, who can be against me?" *(Romans 8: 31)*

Awakening to being established in grace is the sweetest experience I ever had. The reality of the joy and peace abiding in my heart from being established in grace is always there no matter what obstacle or problem I may face.

Suffice it to say that as wonderful as the experience of going to the Crystal Sea was, the grace awakening was even more fulfilling and life changing.

Now that I had these experiences at the Crystal Sea and the grace awakening, I wondered if I should continue to meditate. One of the revelations that came with the awakening of grace was that everything God has for us is a free gift, bought and paid for by the work of Jesus. None of us deserves God's blessings, and we certainly can't earn them. This made meditation feel, in a way, like trying to do something to receive from God.

Jesus Said, "Mark, You Know the Answer"

Sometime later, I was driving across country and began to pray in the Spirit to pass the time. I continued to do this for about four hours. After I arrived at my destination and retired to my room for the evening, I began to pray and found myself back at home, in the spirit, standing on my deck speaking with Jesus. He appeared in the form of a fairly young man, quite different than before. His hair was cut shorter than I expected, He was wearing a white robe and His features resembled those as depicted in the famous painting of Jesus by Akiane Kramarik.

As we were standing on my deck the Lord said to me, "You have a question." I said, "Yes, should I be meditating the way I had in the past?" The Lord replied, shaking His head in mild disappointment, "Mark, you know the answer." He was right. I knew that I should have been seeking Him in the stillness just as before. It hurt to be reminded of my failing.

As suddenly as the Lord appeared, He vanished. I then found myself back where I started, praying in my friend's spare room halfway across the country.

One important lesson I gleaned from this experience was that even though we have all of God in us and with us, we still need to seek more of Him to be released or to be manifested in our lives. If we have believed, confessed and received the Lord Jesus, we already have all of God. The Bible says, *"Whoever confesses that Jesus is the Son of God, God abides in him, and he in God." (1 John 4:17)* This is not to say that the spiritual disciplines aren't important. They are! Bible reading, prayer, and meditation don't appropriate *more* of Jesus for us because we receive Him by grace through faith, it is a gift from God. *(Ephesians 2:8-9)* So why should we care about the spiritual disciplines? They help us *receive* the actual manifestation of the things of the Spirit in this physical world - the things God has already provided for us in the Spirit. As the Bible says in Ephesians 1:3, *"Thanks be to God who has blessed us with all spiritual blessings in heavenly places in Christ."*

By meditating and praying I am not able to get God to give me something or to do something for me. Rather, I am putting myself in a place to receive what He has already made available to me. Another way to say it is that I'm not earning anything; I'm actually discovering what God has had in store for me all along.

Years ago, I heard a story about a man who lived in Europe and wanted to move to America. At that time the only way to travel across the Atlantic was on an ocean liner, a trip that often took over a week. So, he sold all that he had and bought a one-way ticket to America. He only had enough money to buy a little cheese and crackers to sustain him during the voyage.

Each day he would see the other passengers dining on succulent dishes in the various banquet halls and restaurants on the great ship. As he ate his meager fare of cheese and a few crackers, he could overhear their conversations about the beautiful meals they had enjoyed. How he wished that he could have joined them!

Near the end of the trip a fellow passenger noticed that he was sitting outside the dining room and asked if he was coming in. The man replied, "I only had enough money to pay for my ticket. I didn't have enough left over for the meals." The other passenger was astounded and replied, "Young man, the meals were included in your ticket!"

There was a time that I was not walking in the full inheritance that Jesus had provided for me. I knew who Jesus who was; that is, the historical account of His life. Later I came to know Him personally and was confident that I will be with Him in Heaven after I die. But I didn't fully understand the difference my relationship with the Lord Jesus could make now.

I need to always remind myself that Jesus is in me right now by His Spirit and that all of God's promises are because of Him, as well.

Like the man on the ocean liner, we have all that God has to offer in us right now, just waiting for us to wake up and be who we are destined to be. Jesus is knocking on the dining room door and hoping that we will open up and let Him dine with us and us with Him. "*Behold, I stand at the door and knock. If anyone hears My voice and opens the door, I will come in to him and dine with him, and he with Me." (Revelation 3:20)*

I am constantly asking God to help me see the reality of who He says I really am and how I should be living as His son in this world.

Too Good to Be True

I really like what Chuck Swindoll said that relates to the following story, "Grace releases people not only from sin but from shame."

Once I was staying at a hotel with hundreds of other sales people from across the country. I was having dinner with three other company sales reps the night before the first meeting. I really didn't know these folks very well. The gentleman that sat across from me knew that I had recently moved from a sales district in

Hartford, CT, to one in Chicago. He asked, "Why did you move to Chicago?"

I asked if he wanted the short story or the long story. Most people just want to make small talk and really don't want to talk about anything too deep. He wanted to hear the long story, so I told him about my being healed from panic attacks by the power of Jesus and that I moved to Chicago to learn more about God.

You Don't Hate God…You Hate Religion!

His reply startled me as he said, "Mark, I hate God!" Normally I am at a loss for words when I hear something like that, but an inspired reply instantly popped into my mind. "You don't hate God; you hate religion." Now he was just as startled as I had been. He replied, "Aren't they the same thing?" Again, this reply instantly came into my mind, "Religion is mankind's way to relate to God; Jesus is God's way to relate to mankind."

In the morning I went down to breakfast in the courtyard of this huge hotel, expecting to see many people there from my company. The only one there was the gentleman that I spoke with the night before. This in itself was remarkable. We sat down to eat together and he said, "Mark, I hadn't thought about God for years but last night I couldn't stop thinking about Him." I was so blessed that God used me to speak into this man's life. I really wanted to help him see that God loved him. After all, God orchestrated our dinner meeting the previous evening and also our private conversation the next day!

Why Did Jesus Come?

I once thought that if I worked really hard at being the best person I could be, I would gain God's favor. I eventually found out that nothing could be farther from the truth. I ultimately discovered that Jesus didn't come to show us how to live right, how to please God or to tell us about some other thing that we needed to do to get God on our side. None of this makes any sense at all. If our relationship with God is based on our goodness or performance, we are all in big trouble. Jesus explained that the standard God requires of us is perfection when He said, *"Be perfect as your Heavenly Father is perfect." (Matthew 5:48)*

None of us on earth, other than Jesus, ever had a perfect *day* in our lives, let alone a perfect *life*. The only way we can come before a perfect God is to be perfect, and we can only attain perfection if it's given to us as a gift. That's why Jesus came. He came to pay the penalty for what we've done wrong, for all the wrongs done to us, to free us from our sin nature and to credit us with His perfection so that we can come into the presence of a perfect God.

Jesus came to give us the free gift of Himself - His righteousness, love, peace, life, and wealth. All we have to do is receive Him freely by faith. Jesus provided for this at His cross and resurrection over 2,000 years ago. That means that it's already finished, done, final, complete!

Religious bondage comes in when people add us back into the equation. Jesus' free gift of love and acceptance, plus our doing right, actually equals zero. The only way we ever get free from the darkness of this world is by realizing that what Jesus did for us makes us right with God forever. Great joy enters our hearts when we know that we are totally forgiven, loved and accepted by God, not because of what we've done but because of the work of God Himself on our behalf. Jesus paid it all and then gave it all to us.

He Came to Give Us Life

Another reason for Jesus' coming that particularly stands out is from His own words, *"I have come that you might have life and have it more abundantly." (John 10:10)* Jesus came to give His life.

While we were dead in our trespasses and sins, God sent His only Son to give us eternal life. *(Ephesians 2:1)*

Jesus through His death paid for all of our debts between us and God. In addition to providing total forgiveness for our sins, past, present and future by His death on the cross, He has also given us His life through His resurrection from the dead. He gives eternal life, God's kind of life, free of charge to whomever receives Him. *"For if, when we were enemies (with God), we were reconciled to God by the death of his Son, much more, being reconciled, we shall be saved by his life." (Romans 5:10)*

Before He went to the cross, Jesus told His disciples, *"The Holy Spirit that dwells with you shall be in you". (John 14:17)* When Jesus was with them the Holy Spirit was in and with Jesus, and the Holy Spirit was with them, too. With Jesus' resurrection, that changed.

When Jesus rose from the dead after conquering death, sin and the devil, He appeared to His disciples who were in a locked room hiding from those that killed Him. He then breathed on them and said, "Receive the Holy Spirit". In that moment Jesus *recreated* their spirits by breathing His life into them. This was very much like God breathing into the body of the first man, Adam, making him a living soul.

God had started over. When Jesus breathed into His disciples they were born of the Spirit, or *born again*. When we believe in our heart that Jesus is the Son of God and that God raised Him from the dead and confess these beliefs with our mouth, the Holy Spirit breathes His eternal life into our spirit and we become new creatures. We are literally born again, and our spirit is recreated completely new and free from sin in Christ Jesus. The Apostle Paul writes, *"Therefore, if anyone is in Christ, he is a new creation; old things have passed away; behold, all things have become new." (2*

Corinthians 5:17)

When we believe in and receive Jesus, we become a completely new creation! Now as we relate to God, we are no longer just human beings having spiritual experiences. We are spiritual beings having human experiences. This means that we are in Christ and He is in us. *(1 John 4:17)* God is the one who made all this happen. We didn't do anything to earn it, and we certainly don't deserve it. It is a total gift from God, and there can be great joy in the heart of the believer when we truly understand this.

One of the things I didn't realize until later was that I was born into a world that is at war, a great cosmic battle between God and the devil, with humanity caught in the middle. The devil knew he couldn't take on his Creator with a frontal assault, so he attacked God by wresting control of the earth from Adam.

God's answer wasn't a frontal assault either. He didn't want to lose Adam and his descendants in the battle. God conquered the devil in an unexpected way, through weakness. First, God emptied Himself of His divine power and became a man, born as a fragile baby. He lived as a man but without sin, died on a cross for us, and finally rose from the dead, triumphing over death and the devil.

I didn't realize for a very long time that we were just spectators in this, the greatest story ever told. After God conquered the devil on our behalf and took back the earth from his control, He then did something truly amazing. He returned dominion in the earth to us. God did all of this for us, and all we have to do to receive this authority is to believe in Jesus and submit to His authority.

I Awoke to God's Unconditional Love

Once we were visiting some of our closest friends out in the country for a campfire. While sitting around the fire a couple of friends were talking about how we don't have to work or perform to please or appease God. Jesus has already taken away our sin and made us right with God through His sacrifice on the cross. He had also made eternal life available to us as a free gift. They also said that Jesus came to show us God's unconditional love and that He demonstrated this love by His death and resurrection, which had already made us acceptable to God.

I spoke up and said, "God wouldn't have put all those laws, rules and regulations in the Bible if we weren't supposed to keep them." One of my friends asked, "What did the jailor in Philippi do?" I said, "Nothing, he only believed." *(Acts 16:31)*

At that moment something wonderful happened! I felt as if all the sin and guilt of my entire life fell off of me. I suddenly became aware that the heavens were open to me, and now there was no separation between God and me. I also knew that I knew that I was going to heaven when I die. I also felt an indescribable feeling of God's unconditional love and acceptance, plus a sense of joy and peace that were beyond understanding.

After I received the revelation that the heavens were open and that God's love and acceptance were gifts paid for by Jesus, a car pulled into the driveway of the home where we were having the campfire, and someone in the vehicle called out my name three times and drove away in the opposite direction. I took this as a confirmation that God was calling me to go in a different direction, that I would be entering a whole new world, that my life would never be the same and that my relationship with God was going to be very different in the future.

After my initial miracle healing and beginning to seek God wholeheartedly, I began to feel His abiding presence and blessing. After attending church for a while where I began learning many of the Christian do's and don'ts, my awareness of God's tangible presence began to fade. I was told that these rules and regulations would lead me to a closer walk with God, but just the opposite happened for me. My personal experience was that the more I tried to follow religion the farther away God felt. This went on for a number of years, until my encounter with God's grace around the campfire that day.

Before that experience at the campfire, I had been struggling for quite some time with my relationship with God. I was trying with all my might to serve God and to be the best person I could be. I made long lists of my sins, trying my best to overcome them. I was doing everything I could think of to try to become more pleasing to God, but the harder I tried the worse I got.

Even though I was a good person by human standards and it looked on the surface like I had it all together, deep down I didn't feel worthy of being loved by God or anyone else. These deep feelings of guilt, shame and unworthiness persisted, even in the midst of some wonderful experiences with God until I had that encounter with God's unconditional grace and love around the campfire.

This was a supernatural experience unlike anything that had ever happened to me before. It was as if the entire burden I was carrying of all the ways I felt that I let God down or hurt other people no longer separated me from Him. At that moment I realized there were two worlds existing at the same time. My misunderstanding of God and His ways had been keeping me from being aware of this distinction all of my life.

Once I was asked the question, "Do we all have to go under some form of law or personal performance before God can open our understanding to the tangible revelation of His manifold grace?" I really didn't know the answer; but in my experience, it appears to be the case. It seems to me that it would be better to avoid all the rules and regulations that religion wants to put on us from the beginning of our journey with Christ, but I haven't met anyone who has done that. Even the Apostle Paul, who was no slouch when it came to grace, said, *"For I was alive apart from the law once: but when the commandment came, sin revived, and I died."* (Romans 7:9)

Breaking the Law Can Become Irresistible

I found that there is something inside us called the flesh that causes us to rebel against any law, rule or regulation. Yes, people keep certain regulations, partly for fear of the consequences or because they are following a higher law like love your neighbor. There's a human desire that rises up in us when we are told "not to" do something that makes us "want to". Now you can see what Paul meant when he wrote about the law entering and sin reviving. Even if we don't break a rule, that same rule brings our attention right to it, and wanting to break that law becomes irresistible.

A friend of mine wanted to test this theory. His daughter had a few of her friends over for a birthday party. He went out into the yard and told them, "Don't spit on the roses." Then he watched from a distance. Before he gave them that command, they didn't even know the roses existed. Now, not only were the roses the only things they could think about, but spitting on them became almost irresistible. Some wouldn't go near the roses, but they wanted to. Others went over to the roses and wanted to spit on them, but they didn't. Still others went over to the roses in utter defiance, spitting with all the gusto they could muster. What an example of human nature displayed in this little experiment!

Those that stayed far away from the roses are like those of us who won't go anywhere near a certain place or group because "you never know what could happen". The ones who went right up to the roses, so wanting to spit but didn't, are like those of us who commit sins in our hearts but haven't acted them out. Finally, the most stubborn ones are those who don't care about the consequences. No one is going to tell them what they cannot do!

An interesting observation from this experiment might be that people react differently to laws, rules and regulations. Another might be that sin is empowered by the very prohibition that was designed to prevent the behavior. In life, as in this example, sin becomes irresistible when we are told not to do it.

So, how did God empower us to overcome the sin in our lives? God did this by taking away the laws and regulations that were between us and Himself by the cross of Jesus. As the Apostle Paul wrote in his letter to the Colossians: *"And you, He has made alive together with Him, having forgiven you all trespasses, having wiped out the handwriting of requirements that was against us, which was contrary to us. And He has taken it out of the way, having nailed it to the cross." (Col. 2:13a and 14)*

God showed His love for us by sending Jesus to pay the penalty for our sin. Our knowing that God loves us enables us to love Him, which gives us the motivation to follow His ways, not out of obligation but love. God then took away the laws, rules and regulations by nailing them to the cross, rendering sin powerless in our lives. Yes, believe it or not, sin itself is powerless against us. It's the law that gives sin its ability to bring us into bondage. This is because the Bible says, *"Where there is no law there is no transgression." (Romans 4:15)*

Some say God cleaned our slates (the record of our sin debt) through the sacrifice of Jesus on the cross. However, if we tried to keep our slates clean, we would likely mess it up again by breakfast. *He had to do away with the slate* or else Jesus would have had to keep coming back to redeem us every time we fall short. Therefore, God took away the slate by taking away the laws and regulations between us.

Being Truly Free

I now know that I am truly free! But free from what? Are we now free from guilt, condemnation, and shame? Absolutely! Are we free to break every rule and regulation? Actually, yes, but we can't break the law without consequences. God won't punish us for breaking His laws or the government's laws because He doesn't hold them against us. However, the law is still in force here on earth. If we jump off of a six-story building, the consequences will likely prove that the law of gravity is still in force. If we rob a bank, the authorities will enforce certain consequences. Breaking the law will not keep God from loving or accepting us because of what Jesus has done for us. However, these things can harden our hearts toward God and bring painful consequences into our lives. In other words, just because breaking laws, rules and regulations doesn't make God leave us still doesn't mean it's a smart thing to do!

I believe that due to our fallen nature we have to actually experience the futility of our current condition before we are able to change. I've worked with a number of drug addicts over the years; and, to a person, they cannot begin to become free of their addiction until they hit rock bottom. They also never really get free until they surrender their addiction and their lives to a higher power, and the only power I've seen work long term is Jesus Christ. The Bible says, *"The law has become our tutor to lead us to Christ." (Galatians 3:24)* So how does the law lead us to Christ? It leads us to Christ by teaching us the futility of trying to be good enough for God by our performance.

I Tried with All My Might

I wanted to be the best son of God I could be. I found hundreds of laws in the Bible and decided to underline them so that I could focus on keeping them. The more I tried the worse I got. The Bible said to love people the way Jesus loves us. The more I tried, the less patient and loving I became toward others, including my family. I thought that keeping all these rules would make me feel more favored by God, but all I felt was more frustrated and hopeless in my situation. It wasn't until I hit rock bottom that evening at the campfire when I released my burden of trying to be good enough for God, received the grace awakening, and truly felt free.

No one other than God Himself could keep the law perfectly because the law isn't just about doing right or not doing wrong. It's also about our motivation. If we even *want* to break a commandment, God considers that sin. The Apostle Paul wrote, *"But sin seized the opportunity provided by this commandment and produced in me all kinds of sinful desires, since apart from the law, sin is dead."* (Romans 7:8) The law puts us in the hopeless situation of never being able to keep it perfectly, thus leading us to the realization that we need a Savior.

Really, the end of the matter is this - we cannot come to a perfect God due to our imperfections and sin. Therefore, we needed God to come to us with a plan to restore us to our original state of relationship with Him.

God's plan wasn't what we or the devil expected.

After Adam and Eve disobeyed God and were separated from Him, He cursed all of their descendants, declaring them to be sinners. It didn't seem fair to make all of us sinners because of Adam's transgression, but it was a brilliant tactic! Since God declared everyone sinners because of one man's disobedience, He could also declare everyone righteous because of one man's obedience, Jesus Christ. As the Apostle Paul wrote, *"For as by the one man's disobedience the many were made sinners, so by the one man's obedience the many will be made righteous."* (Romans 5:19)

God's plan was to create a masterful equation where the apparent unfairness on one side of the equal sign would justify the unfairness on the other side. It didn't seem fair that we were all made sinners due to Adam's transgression, but it was equally unfair that we could become right with God because of Jesus' obedience. God knew all along that if it was left up to us, we would be lost forever, so He removed us from the equation.

The devil thought that he conquered Jesus when he had him killed on the cross, but he was unaware of this divine equation called the "Great Exchange". By this equation he was defeated, and we were delivered from his power and translated into the Kingdom of God's Son, Jesus Christ. *"He has delivered us from the power of darkness and conveyed us into the kingdom of the Son of His love" (Colossians 1:13)*

The Apostle Paul alludes to the "Great Exchange" principle many times in the Bible. Here's just one example of that equation: *"For our sake He made Him to be sin who knew no sin, so that in Him we might become the righteousness of God." (2 Corinthians 5:21)*

All we have to do is receive with thanksgiving our exchanged nature as a gift from God through Jesus. This is so good it just has to be true!

When I first learned of the Great Exchange, I didn't realize that it included a transfer of power and authority from the Kingdom of God to all believers. I had no idea how badly I would need this Kingdom power and authority until…

8. THE KINGDOM OF GOD AT WORK

The reality of the Kingdom of God invaded my work in an amazing way!

I had been a sales representative in the Chicago area for a major publishing company for almost 14 years. It was 1997 and things were not going very well for me in sales or my income. It felt like I was under attack from every direction. You've probably heard of Murphy's Law: if something can go wrong it will and at the worst possible time. If you want to call him Murphy, bad luck or the devil, that's fine with me. All I know is that I had a huge bullseye on my back during that time, and I was getting hit over and over again.

As the first week of that December was coming to a close, it still seemed like Murphy was working overtime in my business. I had only sold 70% of my annual sales quota with only three weeks left in the year. It was now humanly impossible for me to come back from that far behind. No one had ever sold 30% of their annual sales in that short a period of time before. To top it off, my boss wanted to see me. He probably wanted to remind me that if I finished the year under quota I would be placed on probation; and if I had another bad year, I would lose my job.

My Search for the "One Thing"

It is always cold in December in Chicago, but as I waited in my car I hardly noticed. All I could think about was the dire situation I faced regarding my career. I had many thoughts running through my mind. I've never struggled financially like this before. I had been over quota each of the last 13 years with this company! Why is this happening now? If I lose my job, how will I take care of my family? Finally, I asked, "Where is God in all of this?"

That was the right question. For me the answer, of course, was that He was right there with me. If the King of kings is here as the Bible says He is, then why wasn't His blessing manifesting in my life? So, I pulled my Bible out of the glove compartment looking for answers and began to read the Psalms out loud.

The Kingdom of God Invaded My Heart

A short time later I read Psalm 91, verse 15, *"You shall call upon Me, and I will answer you; I am with you in trouble; I will deliver you."* All of a sudden that statement from the Bible came alive in my heart. "I am with you in trouble. I WILL deliver you!" That was it! God's Kingdom just invaded my heart! I knew that I knew that He was with me in this situation and that everything was going to work out. I broke down and wept in my car, thanking and praising God for His kindness and promised deliverance.

My meeting with my boss was much more encouraging than I had expected, but the most exciting thing was what happened next. On my very next sales call my customer asked me, "How is it going?" I told her, "Honestly, I'm having the worst year of my career." She replied, "How can I help?"

Now I don't recommend that professional sales people follow this type of sales dialogue, but in this instance it worked. I replied, "You could buy something!" I had served this individual faithfully for five years. She controlled one of the largest budgets for information resources in the Chicago-land area, but she never purchased anything from me. Maybe that was because she really liked the guy I replaced and didn't like me because I wasn't him, or maybe she was distracted because her organization spent years building a new facility. Whatever the reason, nothing ever happened on my many visits there...until *that* day.

She then asked, "May I have your catalog?" I handed her my catalog, and she proceeded to buy virtually everything we had! It was one of the biggest orders of my career! After that the financial floodgates suddenly swung open. I could hardly keep up with the pace of the incoming sales. When it was all said and done, I had received over 37% of my annual quota in just three weeks, an impossible feat. I finished 1997 at 107% of my sales target.

I didn't know it at the time but 1997 was my last year as a sales rep for that company. My sales that year weren't worthy of any accolades and didn't set any traditional company records for performance. However, for me it was my most gratifying year because I got to see the power of the Kingdom of God come through, against all odds in the natural, as I put all my trust in Him and as His Word came alive in me.

A Clash of Two Kingdoms

I didn't know that I was up for a promotion at that time. I now understand that the reason why 1997 was so difficult for me was because there were forces in this world that didn't want me to move to St. Louis, MO. We live in a world that is marked by the clash of two kingdoms - the kingdom of darkness and the Kingdom of Light.

I was under such attack from the forces of the kingdom of this world because they knew that if they could get me to give up and succumb to the apparent hopelessness of my situation, they could have blocked my promotion. It was company policy that no one under 100% of their sales quota could be promoted. If they succeeded in keeping me from achieving my sales quota that year, they would have kept me from moving to St. Louis and effectively would have stopped much of the ministry that has come to fruition since then.

I learned a number of lessons from this experience. One was that God cares about everything we need, including our finances. I also discovered at an even deeper level than before that God is at work all around us and is with us in trouble and WILL deliver us.

Something else that became clearer for me after this experience was that in life, as in the Bible, every wilderness is followed by a Promised Land and every Promised Land is followed by another wilderness. That means that in life we will have struggles, but if we keep our trust in God, He will bring us through to a place of rest. On the flip side, if we are in a place of rest, we shouldn't get too comfortable because the forces in this fallen world have a way of bringing new struggles our way.

I didn't enjoy my time in the wilderness, but it was worth it. We learn much more about ourselves in times of struggle than we do when things are going smoothly. There's an old saying that I think fits here: "Great sailors are not made on calm seas". That is so true.

After my wilderness experience in 1997 I stepped into a period of calm seas with the blessings of God all around me. I was asked to take a promotion that was pretty risky because the division I would be managing was in complete disarray. It was also a difficult decision because I would have to leave my current role as part-time pastor of a church that I helped pioneer, the only job I had known for the last 14 years, and my home. I really felt that this was what God wanted me to do, so we moved to St. Louis looking forward to seeing what He would do in this new phase of life.

I felt very underqualified for the challenge I was facing. The task of trying to turn around this struggling sales team that was strewn across 12 states appeared to be humanly impossible. However, God's blessing and guidance were evident throughout this journey.

By the end of 1999 our division went from one of total disarray to leading the nation. To top off that year of blessing, my company gave my wife and me an all-expense paid trip to Hawaii. It really pays to focus on God and His Word to help persevere through the hard times.

I Loved Being a Pastor but Was Still Crying Out to God

A number of years later I left the business world and was working primarily as a pastor of a small church in the suburbs of St. Louis. I really enjoyed my work as a pastor, our church was growing and I was having a lot of fun sharing on the grace and power of God with the congregation.

Even though I thoroughly enjoyed ministering at our church my heart was crying out to God for all the hurting people in our city. I would ask Him, "Is this all there is? We aren't even impacting our neighborhood, let alone our city or nation."

One day my phone rang and the gentleman on the line said, "God told me to tell you that He is closing the door on your ministry at your church, and He is going to move you and greatly multiply your effectiveness for His Kingdom."

Three weeks later I handed the reins of my church over to the associate pastors and walked out of the church I had ministered in for the last seven years, not knowing what was next.

Jesus Is Driving

In order to seek God for direction, I went off by myself to pray in a quiet room in our home. As I was praying, I had a vision that I was walking up to a car idling by the side of the road. I opened the door and Jesus was sitting behind the wheel. He said, "Get in", so I did and off we went. That's all I remember. I think it meant that Jesus was taking me on a journey, and He not only knew where we were going but was also doing the driving.

Sometime later I met a man at a dinner who was speaking about a Gospel proclamation ministry that he had started called *For His Glory Ministries*. His name is Rob Welch. We agreed to meet for coffee to get better acquainted. As we talked, he mentioned having a vision very similar to mine with Jesus driving a car. This was very intriguing for both of us and was, to me, a strong indication that Jesus wanted me to drive off in the ministry, but where?

A big part of *For His Glory's* mission is to share the Gospel at large evangelistic festivals in Africa where tens of thousands of people would become followers of Jesus. But even more important is the ministry's primary focus of training the local churches in any given city to train these new believers on how to make disciples. The cities where these disciple makers have been trained are being transformed by the huge influx of Jesus followers. Authorities in these cities have excitedly shared with me that the jails are emptying, prostitution and crime rates are falling, and the streets are safer at night as more and more people have the influence of Jesus in their lives.

God Points Me to Africa

I was very impressed with the results *For His Glory Ministries* was producing. Up to that time, they had already seen over a quarter of a million people make public commitments to Christ. I agreed to join the Board of Directors while I waited to see where God would take me next. As I was praying again in my quiet room, I had a vision of a beautiful map of Africa painted on parchment, hovering in the air right in front of me.

As this vision faded another came in its place. It was of the warthog from the Disney movie, *The Lion King*. You remember the warthog, Pumbaa, who sang "Hakuna Matata", a song about his worry-free philosophy. I think that the Lord was telling me to go to Africa but, like the warthog, I would be less than excited. I really didn't want to go, so I procrastinated.

Once again, I really needed to seek God about what He wanted me to do about Africa. So, you guessed it! I settled myself back in my quiet room to pray and seek the Lord for direction. God spoke to my heart and said, "Go to Rwanda and you will know."

It just so happened that *For His Glory Ministries* was going on mission to Rwanda in less than a month, so I went.

On the flight to Africa one of the mission team members asked me to lead a workshop on a disciple-making program called Training for Trainers. I replied that I'd rather not because I didn't know anything about Training for Trainers. He explained that he was double-booked and that there wasn't anyone else that could help him out.

He loaned me his book written by the creators of Training for Trainers, Ying Kai and Steve Smith, called T4T-A Discipleship Re-revolution. As I read Ying Kai's story I was impressed, moved and challenged.

Ying Kai was a missionary to communist China who had planted five churches, an impressive feat for even the most effective missionary. Ying felt God was now calling him to reach a city of 20 million people. He knew that he would have to change his church planting approach if he was going to reach a city of that size.

He went away to pray, and the Lord said, "Don't just plant churches, train others to plant churches. Don't just make disciples, train others to make disciples."

After Ying Kai began to train disciples to make disciples, he and his team in just two years planted 3,535 churches with 53,430 water baptisms in China. Over the next eight years he and his disciples planted over 80,000 churches and baptized over 2 million new believers.

By the time we landed in Rwanda I had read enough about Training for Trainers to understand that it was an effective model for spreading the Good News of what God has done for us. Once I saw what was happening already in Africa I was totally on board!

How I Joined the Disciple-Making Revolution

In the fall of 2015, I stepped off the plane in Rwanda, and what I heard and saw revolutionized my perspective on how God wants His Kingdom to advance on earth. On the ride to the hotel in Kayonza, Rwanda, I asked a member of the *For His Glory Ministries* Africa team, "How many Training for Trainers (T4T) disciple makers did you train back in August when T4T was first introduced here?" He told me that they had trained only 165. I asked him, "How many do you have now?" He told me they now had 2,500! That blew me away! "You mean you grew from 165 disciple makers to 2,500 from August to October? That's incredible!" I was sold on T4T.

After reading about what Ying Kai did in China and what the *For His Glory* team accomplished in Rwanda, Africa, I realized that I didn't really practice discipleship the way Jesus designed it; therefore, I wasn't nearly as effective as I could be.

How could I have missed the importance of the last things Jesus said before He left this world, ascending to His throne? He wanted us to realize the significance of making disciples. Jesus told His disciples in Matthew 28:18 – 19 that since all authority had been given to Him in heaven and earth that He wanted them (and us) to go and make disciples of all nations. This means that making disciples of all peoples or nations is one of the things Jesus most wants to happen in this world. It is the way He has directed us to share the Good News that He has taken away our sin and made eternal life available to everyone.

This is a key part of Jesus' message to us, and I totally missed it for years! I had discipled people for decades, which produced some good fruit, but nothing on the scale of what I saw happening through the T4T model.

I asked people to come to church, which is a good thing, but it's not what Jesus said to do. He didn't say "come"; He actually told us to "go". How could I have missed that? I read many times that He wanted us to go make disciples of all nations, but I didn't really know how to do it. Many people have been helped by coming to church over the years, but I could have been much more effective if I understood why Jesus put the emphasis on "go" rather than "come" *(Matthew 28: 19)*. I also discovered that more people will come and join the church if we that are in the church focus first on "going" and then on "coming", in that order.

As I began to focus, even here in the U.S., on "going" to where the people need Jesus, I found myself having many more conversations about Jesus than I ever had before. Others in my groups are doing the same and are now discipling others, as well as leading groups.

Jesus told them and us to teach others to observe His commands, which actually includes His command to teach others *(Matthew 28: 20)*. This means that Jesus was telling us to teach others, who will teach others, and so on. This is Jesus' model of training disciples, and it really works.

We are excited to see the tremendous results that T4T has made in Asia. We are honored that God is using us to help introduce the T4T disciple-making model to Africa. We are already seeing growth here in the U.S as our first T4T disciple-making group of only two people eventually grew to 16 attendees. This group also helped launch over 20 new groups in the St. Louis area in less than 18 months.

This T4T model is so important because it enables us to fulfill the final wishes of the Lord that we be His witnesses here, there, and everywhere. We begin, as Jesus did, by challenging the conventional wisdom of our day. One example is that we flip the conventional model of making disciples from "grow then go" to "grow while you go". We also dispel the belief that only the clergy can do the ministry. Instead, we train church leaders to multiply their impact in the community by empowering their members to do the ministry.

For His Glory Ministries does this by training devoted followers of Jesus how to share their story with their friends, family and social networks. Their story is compelling because that's how God actually became real to them. Their story consists of what their lives were like before Jesus, how they encountered Him, and how their lives have been transformed by His life and love.

This model is revolutionary because it empowers every Jesus follower to share the Good News that God is with us, that He will give our lives meaning and that He will be a potent cure for the pain and miseries we may be encountering. This Training for Trainers (T4T) model is contributing to indigenous, self-perpetuating disciple-making movements here and around the world.

In summary, God is using the Training for Trainers disciple-making model to transfer people from the kingdom of this world into His Kingdom. We will continue to train up disciples of Jesus until the promise of God is fulfilled that the kingdoms of this world have become the Kingdoms of our Lord and Savior.

Even after learning that we live in two kingdoms, my human way of thinking was still in the driver's seat while my spiritual side was in the backseat. One of my earliest childhood memories came flooding back as a good reminder that life goes much better when the Spirit is leading rather than me....

9. THE KINGDOM IS HERE AND NOW

One of my most vivid memories as a child happened when I was about 8 years old. We lived in a first-floor apartment just below our grandparents' flat. Their house was about halfway up one of the steepest hills in our old Connecticut factory town.

Dad must have been feeling prosperous at the time because he bought a boat. It was a sixteen-foot fiberglass runabout, which he kept in Grandpa's garage that was adjacent to their house on that hill.

One day Dad hitched the boat to his 1962 Ford Falcon station wagon and began to pull his trailered boat onto our street, heading down the hill toward the main road. I was seated in the backseat of the station wagon. As I looked to my right out the car window, what I saw blew me away. I was watching in utter amazement as Dad's new boat was rolling down the hill past our car! Obviously, the boat trailer had become unhitched from the car and was heading backwards toward the bottom of the hill.

What a strange sight that was, to see our boat leading our car down the hill toward the bottom of our street.

This story reminds me of the common saying, "putting the cart before the horse." We often let our natural, worldly tendencies lead us in life instead of seeking God so that we can be more influenced by higher, more uplifting aspirations.

Everyone on earth is in the same boat because we all live in this natural world. Unfortunately, just like in my story, the boat, which represents this world with its fallen earthly wisdom, is ahead of the car, God's wisdom. The car, God's Kingdom or His wisdom, should be towing the boat, not the other way around.

The Kingdom of God, which is the realm of the Holy Spirit, should be in the lead in our life, but more often than not He has to take a backseat to the habits we've acquired in this fallen earthly kingdom.

I believe that the remedy is to follow what Jesus said, *"Seek first the Kingdom of God and His righteousness and all these things will be added to you" (Matthew 6: 33)* If we are more focused on the Kingdom of God than this physical kingdom, we will see our thoughts, emotions and actions become more reflective of God's world rather than our own.

I've learned that some people come to a knowledge of the Kingdom of God in a flash of revelation as I talked about earlier, but the vast majority learn the truth of His Kingdom gradually over time. The important thing is that we come to the understanding that God's Kingdom is here, and its power can make a difference in our lives right now.

There are two separate kingdoms existing in this world. One is a physical, earthly realm and the other is called the Kingdom of God, or the Kingdom of Heaven. Most of Jesus' teaching, including the majority of His parables, are about the Kingdom of God. Jesus tried to make people aware of this Kingdom that is beyond this physical world, that He had come from this Kingdom, and He was its King.

At Jesus' trial Pontius Pilate, the governor of the Roman province of Judea, asked Jesus if He was a king. Jesus replied that His Kingdom was not of this world. Jesus later mentioned that He had come to bear witness of this Kingdom, calling it the Truth. The word truth literally means reality, so Jesus was saying that His Kingdom was a realm that was the ultimate reality *(John 18: 33 – 37)*.

I Really Wondered How All This Started

So, this is what God taught me. It was actually in the beginning after God made the heavens and the earth:

"Then God said, 'Let us make human beings in our image, to be like us. They will reign over the fish in the sea, the birds in the sky, the livestock, all the wild animals on the earth.' So God created human beings in His own image. In the image of God, He created them; male and female He created them." (Genesis 1:26-27 NLT)

We can gather from what God said that He wanted to create human beings to resemble Himself for the purpose of ruling the earth and everything in it. Therefore, the first purpose for which we were created was to exercise God's dominion and authority in this world.

God further refines His desire for mankind in the earth when He makes the following statement recorded in the Bible:

"And God blessed them and said to them, be fruitful, multiply, fill the earth, and subdue it [using all its vast resources in the service of God and man]" (Genesis 1:28 AMPC)

I believe that God is telling us that He wants us to be fruitful, multiply, fill the earth and subdue it. The first thing that jumps out at me is that there was something in the earth that needed subduing. That means that something or someone in the earth was opposing God's will for the planet.

God wanted mankind to be the agent through which He would bring the earth in line with His desires and plans for it. We later find out in the Bible that Lucifer and a third of the angels rebelled against God and were cast out of heaven into the earth. These angelic forces were definitely in opposition to God's purposes for the earth. It sounds to me that God wanted mankind to subdue them. I imagine that it really bothered Satan being a powerful archangel and now subject to the authority of beings made of clay such as us.

Jesus spoke to His disciples regarding this in the Bible in *Luke 10: 17 – 19 Then the seventy returned with joy, saying, "Lord, even the demons are subject to us in Your name."*

18. And He said to them, "I saw Satan fall like lightning from heaven. 19. Behold, I give you the authority to trample on serpents and scorpions, and over all the power of the enemy, and nothing shall by any means hurt you."

In using the word "subdue" God wanted mankind to realize that He wanted us to develop the resources He created in the earth to benefit everyone. Using God's creation for the betterment of others is a very high form of service to God and man.

Cover the Whole Earth with the Garden of Eden

Later in Genesis 2:15 we read, *"The Lord God placed the man in the Garden of Eden to tend and watch over it."* Therefore, Adam and Eve were to take care of the Garden. I believe, based on what God had already said, that He wanted them to see to it that the fruitfulness of the Garden of Eden would eventually fill the entire earth with fruit, making the whole earth a garden.

To summarize, God gave dominion over earth and everything in it to mankind. Adam and Eve, the first human beings, were placed in the Garden of Eden. Their purpose was to exercise dominion in the earth and bear fruit. This all sounds like a wonderful way of life. However, there was a problem. Adam and Eve didn't realize that they were placed in a world at war - a war between God and the devil.

Now, fallen angelic beings are no match for God in a direct confrontation. Satan, therefore, attacked God through His agents in the earth, Adam and Eve. Since they had been given authority over everything in the earth, including the devil, he had to attack them through subtlety.

The devil tempted Eve with a lie, implying that God was holding something back from her and Adam. He told them that if they ate of The Tree of the Knowledge of Good and Evil, of which God forbade them to eat, they would not die as God had said but they would be like gods. Ironically, they were made in God's image so they were *already* like God.

The Devil's Favorite Strategy

One of the devil's favorite strategies is to get us to doubt our identity in God. Adam and Eve gave in to the enemy's temptation, and in doing so they disobeyed God. Their rebellion effectively transferred their authority in the earth to Satan. The devil even tried this tactic on Jesus but to no avail. *"Now when the tempter came to Him, he said, "If You are the Son of God, command that these stones become bread." But He (Jesus) answered and said, "It is written, 'Man shall not live by bread alone, but by every word that proceeds from the mouth of God.'" (Matthew 4: 3- 4)*

This rebellion is when the kingdom of this world, Adam and Eve, and all of their descendants were separated from God; and the earth and its inhabitants have been broken ever since. They had now lost all their authority, power and dominion in the earth.

Since then every human being has had an inward yearning for that power to be restored and their brokenness to be healed. Why do people crave money? It's for the power it represents. At our best, we are looking for the power to fix our broken lives; at our worst, we want to control others so that we can feel better about ourselves. However, all the money, power and things of this world cannot replace our loss. Deep down we know that we were made for more - that we are really kings at heart but kings without a kingdom.

Mankind's rebellion broke our connection with God, who is the source of our Kingdom authority. We couldn't return to God to restore our authority because of our brokenness and sin, so God came to us in the person of Jesus of Nazareth. Jesus came to pay the penalty for our rebellion and to reconnect us to God. He also came to give us everlasting life, which is His life. He also came to take back the earth from the devil and restore His Kingdom authority in this world to mankind. As Jesus said, *"Behold, I give you the authority to trample on serpents and scorpions, and over all the power of the enemy, and nothing shall by any means hurt you." (Luke 10: 19)*

Jesus Didn't Come to Establish a Religion but a Kingdom

One really important thing I learned was that Jesus' mission was not to create a religion. It was to establish His Kingdom on earth within the hearts of His followers. Many people think that what Jesus most wanted to accomplish was to get people into heaven when they die. As important as that is, it was not His primary goal. Jesus' primary goal was to get heaven into us!

Jesus told us straight out why He came. *"I have come that they might have life and that they may have it more abundantly." (John 10:10b)* By the way, if you are still wondering what my "one thing" is, it's pretty close to what Jesus just said - that I can have His life and have it more and more abundantly!

Jesus didn't say that He would bring us to a place where there is life. He told us that He was bringing life to us here on earth and that we could have it abundantly. By bringing us life, what was Jesus giving us on earth? The authority to wield His divine power in this world! In John 1:4, John tells us that His (Jesus') life was the light of men. Light is a form of power.

Who stole the earth from Adam and Eve? The Prince of Darkness. What does light have the power to dispel? Darkness. Jesus came to give life, and in His life is the power to restore everything the devil and sin destroyed in this world. We now have a Kingdom of light here on earth with the power to transform the hearts of men into the Kingdom of God. God the Father *"has delivered us from the power of darkness, and has translated us into the Kingdom of His dear Son." (Colossians 1:13)*

At the very beginning of Jesus' ministry, He came to John to be baptized. As He came up out of the water, the Holy Spirit came upon Him and God the Father proclaimed, *"This is my beloved Son, in whom I am well pleased." (Matthew 3:17 KJV)* God said this for everyone to hear, including the devil.

The Holy Spirit led Jesus into the wilderness to be tempted of the devil. Many Bible teachers point to the three temptations the devil used to try and trap Jesus, but there were actually four. Satan tried to get Jesus to question His identity the same way He trapped Eve into thinking she needed to be like God.

The devil's first temptation of Jesus was to question what God said at His baptism by trying to get Jesus to prove He was God's Son, rather than just believing God's word. *"If you are the Son of God, tell these stones to become bread." (Matthew 4:3 NIV)* Jesus didn't need to prove who He was by what He did. He knew who He was. If only we could have that same level of confidence in our identity in Christ! When the reality that we are God's children dawns in our hearts and minds, we become fully operational Kingdom of God ambassadors here on earth.

Our Way of Thinking Needs to Change - God's Kingdom Is Here

I used to think that the word "repent" meant that if I felt sorry enough for my sins and if I promised to do better God would forgive me. I later discovered that "repent" actually means to change the way I think.

After Jesus overcame the devil's temptations, He came up out of the wilderness in the power of the Spirit, proclaiming, *"Repent, for the Kingdom of Heaven is at hand!" (Matthew 3:2 NKJV)*. In other words, Jesus was saying that God's Kingdom power was here and available. All they needed to do, and all we need to do now, is to repent, which means to change our way of thinking from that of the earthly kingdom to that of God's Kingdom.

The Apostle Paul, who wrote much of the New Testament of the Bible, spoke quite emphatically about the need to repent (change our thinking) from human reasoning to a Kingdom mentality.

Here is what he wrote: *"Therefore, I urge you, brothers, on account of God's mercy, to offer your bodies as living sacrifices, holy and pleasing to God, which is your spiritual service of worship. Do not be conformed to this world, but be transformed by the renewing of your mind. Then you will be able to discern what is the good, pleasing and perfect will of God: (Romans 12:1-2)*

So, what should we be renewing our minds to? The fact that if we have surrendered our lives to Jesus and confessed Him as Lord, then He lives in us and will live through us! God wants to rule this planet through the Spirit of His Son Jesus living through His followers.

If Jesus, the King of kings, lives in us, wherever we go the King comes with us; and we have the authority in His name to do what He did to bring forth His will on earth as it is in heaven.

Jesus said, *"All authority in heaven and earth has been given to me." (Matthew 28:18)* Jesus then transferred His authority in the earth to us when He added, *"Go you therefore, and make disciples of all nations." (Matthew 28:19)* When we follow Jesus' command and go out into the world sharing with others what He has done for us, His authority and power is transferred to us through His name so that we can be of help to others in whatever they need.

I don't know about you, but I'm crazy enough to believe that Jesus meant what He said. Jesus went on to say, *"Truly, truly, he that believes in me, the things I do you will do also." (John 14:12)* Therefore, if we believe in Jesus, we should be doing the same works He did. What did Jesus do? He exercised authority over everything in this world. If He was in the midst of a storm that needed to stop, He told it to be calm and it was. When Peter's mother-in-law was sick with a fever, He told it to get out and it left. When we encounter situations in this life that are contrary to God's will in heaven here on earth, we should do what Jesus did and expect the same results.

When I wake up each morning, I ask God to fill me with the tangible presence of His Spirit, to include me in what He is doing that day, to send me across someone's path whom His Spirit has specifically prepared, and enable me to make a difference in their life by introducing His Kingdom to them through His Son. Since I've been doing this regularly, I've been seeing the power of God's Kingdom manifesting in the lives of others every day.

I hope you will do this as well; if you do, you will experience the Kingdom of God right here and now.

Life's Most Burning Question

In thinking about God's sacrificial love for me, I was wondering how to convey God's kind of love because it is so opposite the kind of love we experience in this world's kingdom. I have learned that the Kingdom of God is all about demonstrating His kind of selfless love to love-thirsty people in this hurting and fallen world.

What Is Love?

Business Insider reported in an article entitled "10 Burning Questions That People Asked Google" was that the number one question people wanted answered was "What is love?" That simple question beat out questions like "What is gluten?" and "What is Twitter?"

Isn't that strange? With all the references to love in music, media and movies you would think that everyone would know what love is; but we don't!

While in high school I met a young lady in study hall. She says she fell in love with me while we played cards in the school cafeteria. I fell in love with her when I saw her walking down the school hallway with her long, beautiful hair swaying as she moved ever so gracefully. I said to myself, "I love this woman and she's going to be mine."

Is this love or merely infatuation? This is the only kind of love many people will ever know. Fortunately for me this lovely lady did become my wife, and we grew to experience love in a way that was much deeper and fulfilling.

Unfortunately, the word love is used indiscriminately in our language and culture. We say we love our spouses, our cars, vacations and even ice cream. To hear us talk you would think that we love them all the same way. We touched on this briefly in a previous chapter; but since this is such an important subject and the foundation for God's Kingdom on earth, we'll do a little deeper dive here.

Many English words find their origin in other root languages like Latin, Greek and Hebrew. The Greek language is much more precise than English. For example, there are a number of Greek words for love. The most common word in the Greek lexicon for love is "eros", where we get the English word erotic. This word for love, then, means a strong desire to possess something or someone for our own selves or selfish pleasure. It can mean infatuation, sexual desire or lust. Eros was used quite extensively in ancient Greek plays.

The other commonly used word for love in Greek was "phileo", or brotherly love. The city of Philadelphia derives its name from this Greek word and is why it's known as the City of Brotherly Love. Phileo is love that is felt for another person. This kind of love can be quite tangible. It can create a very powerful bond among family members and tribes. It's likely the highest form of love a human being can feel for another person apart from the supernatural love of God.

The third word for love from the Greek language that we will touch on is "agape". This word for love was not used in any Greek literature or plays that we know of. It was as if God had coined the word and set it aside in the Greek dictionary, waiting for the time He would define its meaning through the sacrificial life of Jesus Christ.

The Highest Form of Love

The highest form of love is this Greek word "agape". It's the kind of love that has its origin in God and is typified by selfless, unconditional love for another. This is the kind of love that God has for everyone. It is also the kind of love we experience when we realize that God loved us so much that He gave His only Son to be crucified for us.

When I think about God's kind of love I am reminded of the movie, *The Finest Hours*. There were a number of heroic characters in this true story, but the one who most epitomized selfless love was Coast Guard Captain Bernie Webber, played by actor Chris Pine.

During the bitterly cold winter of 1952 a violent storm hit the New England coast. This Nor'easter was so severe that it literally tore in half a huge oil tanker that was headed for Boston, stranding over 30 men on the rapidly sinking tail end of the ship.

Captain Webber and three other seamen headed out into the storm in freezing conditions in a small, under-powered wooden lifeboat. Against all odds they found the stranded hulk and began to rescue the exhausted sailors one-by-one, an extremely difficult task in such high seas.

Their small craft was built for 12 passengers plus the crew. By the time they had rescued 22 of the tanker's men, the wooden lifeboat was taking on water. The moment that most exemplifies to me agape love (God's selfless love) in the movie was when a crew member said to Captain Webber, "We're so heavy now we can't even steer. There must be seven or eight more guys up there. Maybe we take these in and come back out?" What Captain Webber said next was truly selfless. "Can't leave them out here alone, that boat won't last; we all live or we all die." Captain Webber and his crew went on to save all 32 souls, accomplishing the greatest small boat rescue in American history!

Jesus said, *"Greater love hath no man than this, that a man lay down his life for his friends." (John 15:13 KJV)* That is the definition of agape love, to put the welfare of others before our own. That's exactly what Captain Webber and his crew did for those men that fateful night. That's also what Jesus did the day of His crucifixion. He loved us so much that He laid down His own life that we might be forgiven and have access to His eternal life.

I have found that human love was not strong enough to enable me to forgive some of the people who hurt me over the years. I really need God's kind of sacrificial love to be able to forgive them. The best part of forgiving the people who have wounded me is that I'm actually freeing *myself* from my own burdens of hurt, anger and bitterness.

Jesus knew that in His final hours He would need to draw from His reservoir of divine love to be able to forgive those who would nail Him to a cross and His closest friends who abandoned and denied Him.

Just before Jesus was going to go to His trial and death on the cross, He told His disciples, *"Where I am going you cannot follow me now". Peter said to Jesus, "Lord why can I not follow you now? I will lay down my life for your sake." (John 13:36-37) Jesus replied, "Will you lay down your life for my sake? Truly, truly, I say to you that before the rooster crows this morning, you will have denied me three times." (John 13:38)*

After this scene, Jesus was praying in a nearby garden when a number of soldiers came and led Him away to the high priest's house. His disciples Peter and John followed from a distance. Somehow, they gained entrance to the courtyard of the high priest's house. Maybe they sold fish to the family or knew the kitchen staff. One way or another, both John and Peter were within earshot of Jesus' trial before the high priest.

In Jewish custom a defendant could ask for others to speak on his behalf during the trial. Peter and John, two of Jesus' most intimate friends, stood closely enough to Him to hear as Jesus said, *"Ask them which heard me, what I have said unto them: behold, they know what I said." (John 18:21 KJV)* This was a request for Peter and John to stand up for Jesus, but they refused to say anything in His defense.

I have that found that what happened next was even worse. During Jesus' interrogation by the high priest, three separate people asked Peter if he knew Jesus. Peter denied knowing Him each time, just as Jesus had foretold. The third time the Bible recounts that Peter not only denied knowing Jesus but that he even cursed that he did not know the man. In that moment, Jesus turned and looked at Peter, and the Bible says that Peter went out and wept bitterly.

Jesus knew that Peter would betray Him. However, I believe that knowing beforehand and actually experiencing it have a very different impact emotionally. I contend that when Jesus saw His two friends deny Him, John by his silence and Peter by his fervent denial, it had to have hurt Him deeply. When Jesus turned and looked at Peter in the midst of his swearing that he didn't know Him, what anguish and hurt Peter must have seen in Jesus' face!

Peter's and John's love for Jesus was the human kind. It was the brotherly love, or phileo, at best. Jesus' love for them and us is far deeper because He forgave them and us and proved it by laying down His life. Peter and the other disciples of Jesus could not have loved Him with Jesus' love because agape love comes only from God.

After Jesus rose from the dead He appeared to His disciples and breathed on them, saying that they would receive the Holy Spirit and whoever's sins they forgave would be forgiven. It was at that moment that Jesus' disciples became new creatures. They were now physical beings with a new, recreated spirit that was one with the Holy Spirit. This meant that they now had the capacity by the power of the Spirit to forgive everyone who had ever hurt them.

They could now love God, themselves, each other and even their enemies with God's unconditional love.

The Bible says, *"This is love: not that we have loved God, but that He loved us and sent his Son to be the payment for our sins." (1 John 4:10 GWT)* What this means is that we can only love with God's love when we have a revelation of His love for us. How do we come to such a revelation? We come to an understanding of God's immense love for us through a realization that God has paid for our sins and cancelled all of our debts through the atoning sacrifice of His Son Jesus.

This revelation is the doorway to an intimate relationship with God. Once we realize that there's nothing we can do to get God to love us more, and there's also nothing we can do to make Him love us less, we rest in Jesus' work for us through His cross and resurrection. We stop trying to appease God and settle into the reality that He loves us because of who He is and not based upon our performance. This enables us to rest in God and just enjoy each other's presence and companionship - in a word, love.

Peter's Intimacy with the Lord Restored

There's a very interesting conversation between Jesus and Peter after Jesus' resurrection and shortly before He left the earth to be with His Father.

After they all dined on the beach, Jesus said to Simon Peter, "Simon son of Jonas do you love (agape) me more than these (my other disciples)?" He (Simon Peter) replied, "Yes, Lord you know that I love (phileo) you. Jesus, replied, "Feed my lambs".

Then a second time, Jesus said, "Simon son of Jonas, do you love (agape) me?" He replied, "Yes, Lord you know that I love (phileo) you." Jesus then replied, "Feed my sheep."

Then a third time Jesus asked Simon Peter, "Simon son of Jonas do you love (phileo) me?" At this point Peter was grieved that Jesus asked him a third time, do you love me. Peter then said, "Lord, you know all things, you know that I love (phileo) you. Jesus then said, "Feed my sheep." (John 21:12-17)

There is a lot happening in this intimate conversation between Peter and the Lord. One of the first things you may notice is that Jesus asked Simon Peter if he loved Him three times, the same number of times Peter denied Him. It was as if Jesus was tying the fact that He already forgave Peter for denying Him to Peter's ability to love. As I mentioned before, our ability to love selflessly is a direct result of our revelation of God's gift of total forgiveness. Jesus, God in the flesh, was showing Peter that he was forgiven, loved and worthy of being part of His plan for the world going forward.

It's also quite telling that Jesus called Simon Peter by his original name in this instance, Simon son of Jonas. Simon was his name before Jesus changed it to Peter, which was after he received the revelation of the divinity of Jesus by God the Father. I believe Jesus called him Peter, which meant rock, because he had received a revelation that Jesus was the foundation and chief corner stone of the Church, the people of God on earth. Peter quite literally had a piece of Jesus, the Rock.

Jesus used the name Simon, which means "to listen attentively", because He wanted him to do just that, listen and learn about love. Jesus wanted Simon Peter to understand His kind of selfless, agape love so that he could teach His new converts (lambs) and His followers (sheep).

The first time Jesus asked Simon Peter, "Do you love me?" He used the Greek word agape for love. When Simon responded, he used the Greek word phileo for love because it was the finest type of love he knew. Jesus was leading him to a place where he could begin to receive a higher revelation of God's unconditional love.

When Jesus asked Simon the second time, He used the Greek word agape again, and Simon responded again with the Greek form of phileo love, which is the kind of love and closeness we have for friends and family.

The third time Jesus asked Simon if he loved Him, Jesus met Peter where he was and used the Greek word phileo for love. Simon responded with the word phileo, emphatically confirming that Jesus knew that Simon loved Him.

I believe that Peter must have thought about this conversation with Jesus about love countless times over his remaining years. I also believe that his continual pondering of the meaning of agape love ultimately enriched his writings and ministry.

So, what is love? Well, God's kind of love, agape, is the practice of putting the welfare of others before that of ourselves. This is impossible for human beings to do in our own strength. We actually have to draw upon God's ability to love others more than ourselves, and when we do love others by tapping into God's power and love we get a glimpse of His miracle-working power displayed in our everyday lives.

As I see my relationship with God grow, my ability to love and forgive others and myself grows proportionately. I also see His abundant life and influence breaking through other barriers, such as my finances, which we will discuss in the next chapter.

10. ABUNDANCE IS A WAY OF THINKING

Back in the early 1980's I was experiencing God's blessing in my work and family life, but I wanted more of God and His abundance in my life. I felt that God wanted me to move to Chicago to be mentored by the pastor that God used to heal me through that flash of divine light. His name was John Scudder, a retired aeronautical engineer who became a pastor and well-known healer.

Pastor John had seventeen patents over his career as an engineer, but he is best known for a dry ice pellet machine that makes it possible for passengers to have cold drinks on commercial flights. Before John's machine became available, a passenger could only get coffee, tea or water during a flight.

John frequently used this invention as an example of abundant thinking in his sermons and conversations. Here was a machine that conventional wisdom said couldn't exist because you can't compress dry ice without the intense cold shattering the device itself. But here it is, a concrete miracle and a testament to God's Kingdom thinking and blessing. John's impossible machine is in airports all over the world and has been blessing travelers for years. *"With God all things are possible." (Matthew 19: 26)*

Pastor John was also known as a healer, a fact I can attest to since

My Search for the "One Thing"

God healed me from severe panic attacks through him. People came to John's home from all over the world to be healed. One of the people who was healed through his ministry was featured on the 1970's show, *That's Incredible*. However, I didn't seek John's mentorship because of his healing ministry; I was looking to learn more about the Kingdom of God and how its power works here on earth.

If we were to move to Chicago, the first thing I needed to know was whether or not Pastor John would be willing to mentor me. To find out, we scheduled a family vacation to the Midwest in August of that year and spent some time at the pastor's home in Chicago. I asked him if he would take me on as a disciple, and he agreed.

The next thing I needed was a job if we were going to be moving out west. During that same vacation, I decided to pay a visit to my company's office in the Chicago area to let them know that I would be open to a job there if one should come available in the near future. As I walked into the Chicagoland office the manager was actually interviewing someone for a sales position there. He knew that I was a successful representative working out of the Boston office and kiddingly asked me if I wanted a job. My reply surprised him when I said, "Yes". He subsequently offered me a position in his region, and my job transfer to the Chicago Region was initiated.

We saw God's favor in the process of finding a job halfway across the country, and He blessed us in the selling of our home in Connecticut as we prepared to move. This was long before the Internet or computers, when most homes were sold by local realtors through newspaper advertising or by word of mouth. I decided to tap into God's Kingdom to sell our home, so I prayed and placed an ad in the local paper. Within a few short hours of the newspaper hitting the streets a buyer came to tour our home and bought it on the spot! What a blessing to have sold our home so quickly.

We visited Chicago in mid-August, and by October 1st of that same year our family moved to our new home in Illinois. Only by God's abundant blessing were we able to sell our home in Connecticut, move 1,000 miles to a new home, in a new city, and already have employment lined up, in six short weeks! Now I was able to work during the day to provide for my family and work on my ministry training in the evenings. I also had the bonus of regular one-on-one mentoring visits with my new pastor, which were tremendous times of spiritual growth and maturing for me.

The blessings didn't stop there, though. After moving to the Chicago area, my personal sales performance at work began to skyrocket. It couldn't be just because of me that my sales began to take off because I didn't become that much better of a salesman on the drive across the country. I believe that it was largely the flow of God's favor and blessing on my work that made the difference. Of course, I had to work hard, but almost everything I did at work went my way. I eventually led my entire sales region and division that year.

To cap off God's blessings on my work that year, the company actually gave my wife and me an all-expense paid trip to Hawaii. I was told that this award was an acknowledgement of my superior sales performance that year, having finished in the top ten nationally. However, the real reason for the exceptional sales production I experienced at that time was largely due to God's blessings flowing through me into my work.

I had the honor to be mentored by John for over five years until it was time to step out in ministry on my own. John was a tough taskmaster and very hard on me and others at times, but I always knew he loved me and had my best interests at heart. I am grateful for the time I spent with him and for the many things I learned.

In moving to the place God had called me to be, I was placing myself in a position where the flow of His life, favor and blessing became tangible here on earth. The Kingdom of God was manifesting more fully in my earthly existence than ever before. When we are in tune with the Spirit of God, abiding in His presence and listening to His voice, the flow of God's blessing on our lives becomes evident and the glory of God becomes a reality around us.

As I began to act in concert with what God was telling me to do, I found that the flow of His blessing in my life was gaining momentum. I began to observe that the law of scarcity was being suspended around me by a higher law called the *"Law of the Spirit of Life in Christ Jesus" (Romans 8:2)*. Christ in me was producing the abundant life I so longed for, and it was becoming evident to people all around me that something special was going on.

I have found it to be true that God has blessed every human being on earth. As the Bible says in Matthew 5:45, *"To show that you are the children of your Father Who is in heaven; for He makes His sun rise on the wicked and on the good, and makes the rain fall upon the upright and the wrongdoers alike"*. God has provided in His creation enough wealth for every human being to live an abundant life here on earth. That was certainly true when He placed Adam and Eve in the Garden of Eden, and it is just as true for us today. The problem in the world in which we live is that the brokenness of humankind has turned the abundance of God (made available to us in His creation) into a domain typified by scarcity.

God's very nature is directly opposed to scarcity. Just look at the breadth and diversity in creation with billions of species of plants and animals, not to mention the countless stars in the heavens or the grains of sand by the seashore. God has built fruitfulness and multiplication right into the fabric of His creation. When He made mankind, He blessed them, telling them to be fruitful and multiply and fill the earth. Everything God blesses multiplies its fruitfulness. One example is an acorn. Not only does one small acorn have a whole oak tree in it, but there is also an entire forest in that one seed. God blessed the seed-bearing trees in the beginning, and they have been multiplying ever since.

If God has already blessed us with abundance, why do so many of us struggle just to survive or to "make ends meet"? It's because of our thinking. We have inherited the scarcity mindset of this fallen earthly kingdom, and we have not yet had our thinking transformed by the renewing of our minds to the abundance available through the Kingdom of God. *(Romans 12:2)*

Again, the system of this world is one of scarcity. The very definition people use in this world for economics reflects a mindset of lack. For example, the definition most often used in school for economics is "the study of the distribution of scarce goods and services".

Just look around and you will observe people everywhere using scarcity strategies to control others for financial gain. They do this by rationing resources and by limiting access, such as tickets to a movie theater, seats at a ballgame, the limited number of tickets for a commercial flight, and so forth. We need to move our thinking from one focused on lack and limitation to one focused on the God of abundance.

Jesus told us to share the good news of His Kingdom to all the nations of the world. When this is accomplished, we will see the people of the world move from the current era of scarcity to an age of abundance. No matter what situation we find ourselves in, we can begin to move more and more into the stream of God's favor and abundance by renewing our minds to the fact that unlimited possibilities are available through Him.

After all, *"His divine power has granted to us all things that pertain to life and godliness, through the knowledge of him who called us to his own glory and excellence"*. *(2 Peter 1:3)*

Jesus Came to Give Us Abundant Life Here and Now

I'm not saying that if we focus on God and abide in His presence that we'll never have any trouble. In fact, just the opposite happens many times. I believe this is due in part to the fact that we live in a broken world that is very resistant to change. Also, the devil, who is the author of scarcity, does not want us tapping into God's abundance. The Bible contrasts the world's system of lack with God's system of abundance in the following words of Jesus: *"The thief comes only to steal and kill and destroy; I have come that they may have life, and have it more abundantly."* (John 10:10)

After God created Adam and Eve, He told them that they could eat of all the trees in the Garden. That's abundance! God told them to avoid just one tree - The Tree of the Knowledge of Good and Evil. The devil introduced scarcity into this world by convincing Adam and Eve to eat of that tree. They took their focus off of God and the abundance He had provided and narrowed their attention to just one tree, ushering scarcity into the human race.

The problem was not only that Adam and Eve disobeyed God by eating of the Tree of the Knowledge Good and Evil. It was also that the fruit they ingested was poison, and that poison has subsequently infected all their descendants.

The scarcity mentality resulting from the fall of humankind has led us to play right into the hand of the Thief. Instead of enjoying the abundant life that Jesus came to give us, most of us are competing with each other for what is perceived to be scarce resources. Some will even steal, kill and destroy to get "theirs" at the expense of others. Jesus made abundance available to everyone. Most aren't aware that it's here, and many that do know that abundance has been provided don't know how to appropriate it.

To walk in God's abundance, we must first realize that we can't make God give to us. Trying to obligate God by something we do is not Biblical and is a misunderstanding of the Truth. The Bible records God as saying, *"Who hath first given unto me, that I should repay him? Whatsoever is under the whole heaven is mine." (Job 41: 10)*

The prosperity gospel and the "give to get" messages are perversions of the true Biblical instruction regarding generosity, giving and abundance. We don't give to get from God. We acknowledge that all we have comes from Him. We are already blessed and abundance is our heritage.

The doorway to an abundant life is generosity. However, we are not generous to be blessed; we are generous *because* we are blessed. We know that we can't out-give God. We don't give to get; we give because we are in the flow of God's blessing, and the more we give the greater His abundance flows through us.

In summary, we are blessed to be a blessing.

How We Think Is Even More Important

In much of this book I shared about how our perception of God and His Kingdom on earth effects the quality of our lives here and now. Pastor John used to quote this, *"For as a man thinks in his heart, so is he..." (Proverbs 23:7a)*, all the time. I mean ALL the time! It took me years to realize what he was trying to help me understand. I believe what he was saying was that as important as it is to be careful about *what* we think about, *how* we think is even more important.

As we discussed in previous chapters, we live in two kingdoms.

We were created by God for abundance and to function as His child in an intimate relationship with Him.

Due to the fall of mankind, the world's inhabitants have had their hearts darkened by their separation from God. As the Apostle Paul points out regarding our minds being darkened, *"But even if our gospel is veiled, it is veiled to those who are perishing, 4. whose minds the god of this age has blinded, who do not believe, lest the light of the gospel of the glory of Christ, who is the image of God, should shine on them." (2Corinthians 4: 3 – 4)*

We no longer think in our hearts from a place of life and abundance but from scarcity and self-centeredness. Jesus came to restore all that was lost, destroying the works of the devil and making God's life and light available to every heart that is open to receive Him. *"For this purpose, the Son of God was manifested, that He might destroy the works of the devil." (1John 3: 8b)*

One of the most important things to remember about walking in abundance is that we have already been given all of God's blessings in the Spirit in Christ Jesus. *"Blessed be the God and Father of our Lord Jesus Christ, who has blessed us with every spiritual blessing in the heavenly places in Christ." (Ephesians 1:3)*

In addition, every promise of God is already ours through Christ. *"If you belong to Christ, then you are Abraham's seed, and heirs according to the promise." (Galatians 3:29)*

God has restored us to everlasting life and has given us life even more abundantly through Jesus Christ our Lord. *(John 10:10)* To walk in this abundant life, all we need to do is to believe that Jesus made us worthy to receive it by His blood and have an active expectation that God will do all that He has promised.

The author of the Biblical book of Hebrews ties faith and expectancy together quite well: *"But without faith it is impossible*

)r he who comes to God must believe that He is,
rewarder of those who diligently seek Him."
e that this verse is telling us that by faith we can
cting to receive.

In summary, here is the way we should be thinking in our hearts about the Kingdom of God:

1. We are righteous before God, not because of what we've done but because of what Jesus has done for us.

"For He (God) has made Him (Jesus), who knew no sin, to be sin for us; that we might be made the righteousness of God in Him." (2 Corinthians 5:21)

2. All the blessings of God are already ours in Christ.

"Blessed be the God and Father of our Lord Jesus Christ, who has blessed us with all spiritual blessings in heavenly places in Christ." (Ephesians 1:3)

3. God's provision comes from an intimate relationship with Jesus Christ.

"According as His divine power <u>has given unto us all things that pertain unto life and godliness, through the knowledge (intimacy) of Him</u> who has called us to glory and virtue." (2 Peter 1:3)

4. The blessing of God, not our performance, brings abundance.

"The blessing of the LORD brings wealth, without painful toil for it." (Proverbs 10:22)

5. A generous heart is a key to an abundant life.

"But seek you first the kingdom of God, and His righteousness; and all these things shall be added unto you." (Matthew 6:33)

6. Ask God for His abundance to manifest in our lives - not just for our needs but to be a blessing to others and to further His Kingdom in the earth, without doubt, expecting to receive.

"You do not have, because you do not ask. You ask and do not receive, because you ask wrongly, to spend it on your passions." (James 4:2b – 3)

7. When the reality of God's abundance from His Word becomes more tangible in our hearts than the reality of the scarcity mentality that has been programmed into our hearts by the world, God's abundance will begin to manifest more and more in our lives.

"Now faith is the substance or assurance of things hoped for, the evidence or conviction of things not seen," (Hebrews 11:1)

Jesus Declares His Kingdom

Everything we have discussed in this book begins and ends with Jesus Christ. So, let's conclude by looking briefly at what He did.

Jesus did not just come to get us into heaven; He also came to get heaven into us.

He did not come to bring a religion; He came to establish the Kingdom of God in our hearts.

He came to destroy the works of the devil and to bring life more abundantly.

He came to reestablish God's dominion in the earth through those sons of men who were also born of the Spirit.

Jesus, the King of Kings, began His earthy ministry by first preaching, "Repent, for the Kingdom of Heaven is at hand". *(Matthew 4:17)* In saying this, Jesus was beginning to declare how radically different His Kingdom would be from the kingdom of this world. He was saying that we need to repent (change our thinking) from the world's way to the way of God's Kingdom.

Immediately after Jesus overcame the temptations of the devil in the wilderness He returned to Nazareth in the authority and power of the Spirit. He then openly declared what His Kingdom would look like and what He came here to do in Luke 4:16 – 21:

So, He (Jesus) came to Nazareth, where He had been brought up. And as His custom was, He went into the synagogue on the Sabbath day, and stood up to read. [17] And He was handed the book of the prophet Isaiah. And when He had opened the book, He found the place where it was written:

[18] "The Spirit of the LORD is upon Me,
Because He has anointed Me
To preach the gospel to the poor;
He has sent Me to heal the brokenhearted,
To proclaim liberty to the captives
And recovery of sight to the blind,
To set at liberty those who are oppressed;
[19] To proclaim the acceptable year of the LORD."

[20] Then He closed the book, and gave it back to the attendant and sat down. And the eyes of all who were in the synagogue were fixed on Him. [21] And He began to say to them, "Today this Scripture is fulfilled in your hearing."

Jesus declared that He was anointed with kingship authority and power to do the following:

To preach the Gospel (Good News) to the poor because only the "poor in spirit" are hungry for more of the Spirit and open to receiving the Kingdom of God in their hearts. *(Matthew 5:3)*

To heal the brokenhearted because their woundedness creates an openness to God's presence and healing power. The brokenhearted who surrender their brokenness to Jesus as Lord have a humbleness that makes them usable for His Kingdom. *(James 4:6)*

To proclaim liberty to the captives because Jesus by His death and resurrection has set us free from sin, death, the flesh, the bondage of this world and the devil. Jesus *has* delivered us from the power of darkness, and we *have been* translated into His kingdom. *(Colossians 1:13)* We are now free to know God, His love for us and to love Him freely in return.

To recover sight to the blind because Jesus opened the eyes of those that were blind physically and spiritually in order to be able to see the Kingdom of God. *(John 3:3)*

To set at liberty those that were oppressed by freeing us from the oppression of the devil and of this world system. Jesus conquered the world on our behalf and deprived it of its ability to harm us. *(Galatians 5:1) (John 16:33)*

To proclaim the acceptable year of the Lord, referencing the year of Jubilee where all slaves were set free and all debts were forgiven. Jesus came to bring us this Jubilee because He has totally freed us from the bondage of sin and the flesh and cancelled all our debts between us and God. *(Psalm 103:1 – 4 and 1 John 4:10)*

In Conclusion

We began our journey together by pointing to a quest to find the "one thing". You have probably surmised what that is for me and hopefully are closer to knowing the "one thing" that God has for you.

It is important to remember that the "one thing" is more about who you are than what you do.

As a follower of Jesus my "one thing" is my relationship with Him and my body being one of His dwelling places here on earth. Through my relationship with the Lord Jesus, I have received His life and receive more of His life abundantly every day.

We are also called to be a gift to the world, to use our gifting to be of benefit to others and to further His Kingdom in this world.

My hope is that what I shared in this book will have been a blessing and an inspiration to you.

At the very beginning of this book I mentioned a scene from the movie *City Slickers* where the old cowboy Curley asked Mitch, "Do you know what the secret to life is? It's just one thing. You stick to that and nothing else matters." Mitch responds, "That's great, but what's the one thing?" Curley then says, "That's what you've got to figure out!"

My prayer is that God will lead you to find your "one thing" and that you will find greater meaning and purpose as God's Kingdom becomes more of a reality in your life.

I hope that we will one day meet, either in this world or in the next. Until then, have an awesome journey with the Lord!

(All Bible references are quoted in the New King James Version unless specified otherwise.)

ABOUT THE AUTHOR

Mark is an accomplished speaker, teacher, and writer. He has trained and mentored ministry and business leaders in numerous nations in Africa, the United Kingdom and in the United States.

Mark began training pastors and church leaders internationally in 2015. To date, he has helped train over 250,000 people in Training for Trainers, Kingdom multiplication, church planting, and discipleship.

Mark and his wife Kathy have two married sons and four grandchildren.